NOTE FOR THE R

MW01098411

Sahifa-e-Sajjadiya comprises of heart touching supplications given to us as a gift from our beloved Imam Ali Ibn Al Hussain.

To be honest, I would read Sahifa-e-Sajjadia rarely; only if it would be mentioned to read a particular supplication in some salat to be read on special holy days. This was mainly because of its inaccessibility as an easy read.
Most books that I would find are in Arabic. English is a language most easily understood by many. Hence the thought of compiling these beautiful supplications in a commonly used, global language arose. It's amazing how when Allah decides to bless you, he will cause situations to come together in your favour.

This compilation, in the form of a beautifully coloured and designed book, is a humble step towards reaching out to people who can make these supplications a part of their routine read and put them to good use in their daily lives.

We wish our readers a happy read!

"Be thankful for the unknown blessings already on their way"

Compiled with Love
by
S. Anwar & A. Jillani

Sahifa al Sajjadiya
The Book of Sajjad

A celebrated collection of supplication and whispered prayers attributed to Imam Zayn-al-ʿĀbedin, the great grandson of Prophet Muhammad (s.a.w). His father was Imam Husayn ibn Ali (a.s) and his mother was a noble Persian known as Shahrbanu.

Ali Ibn al Hussain has been given two titles ; Zayn al-Abidin meaning "Adornment of the Worshippers" and Al-Sajjad meaning "The Consistently Prostrating".

Imam Ali ibn Husayn is most known for his presence in Karbala on the10th of Muharram when his father, Imam Husayn, was martyred along with his family and companions. Imam Ali ibn Husayn'sextreme illness on that day resulted in his inability to participate in the battle, leaving him unharmed by the enemy. Though that was just the beginning of the horrors that he was yet to face when he, the only male survivor along with his female relatives and companions of the Ahlul Bayt were taken captive and forced to walk from Karbala, Iraq, to the palace of Yazid in Damascus. This traumatic journey, bravely facing Yazid in his court, delivering his historic sermon in Umayyad mosque as he condemned Yazid's crime of massacring the progeny of the Prophet, and finally, returning home to Medina with a grievedcaravan, enabled him to be a living history of Karbala and uphold the role of Imamate after his father.

The Imam had a long period as Imam (34 years). From 61 A.H until 95 A.H, he was known forhis discipline and commitment to Allah. In addition to his impeccable qualities, the Imam spent much of his life supplicating to God and prostrating to Him.

Universally acknowledged as an enthusiast of worship and prayer, it is not surprising that an extensive amount of devotional material is associated with his name. During his tenure, the Imam wrote many works which served to revive some of the religious knowledge of the Prophet (s.a.w) to the followers of Ahlul Bayt in particular and Muslims in general.

Al-Sahifa al-Sajjadiyya is an example of the highest form of eloquence.According to Shia narrations, the book is said to have been composed after the Battle of Karbala (680 AD) and describes the relationship between man and God.

Shia tradition considers this book with great respect, ranking it behind the Quran and Ali's Nahjal-Balagha. These beautiful supplications of Imam Sajjad are sure to touch the hearts and re-kindle the spark of faith in many souls.

"Remember that the most precious thing you hold in this world is your heart, so do not let anything taint your heart"- Imam Sajjad

The Treasury

S01 - In Praise of God

When he (upon him be peace) began to supplicate, he would begin with praise and laudation of God (Mighty and Majestic is He). He would say:

Praise belongs to God,
the First, without a first before Him,
the Last, without a last behind Him.
Beholders' eyes fall short of seeing Him,
describers' imaginations are not able to depict Him.

He originated the creatures through His power with an origination,
He devised them in accordance with His will with a devising.

Then He made them walk on the path of His desire,
He sent them out on the way of His love.
They cannot keep back
from that to which He has sent them forward,
nor can they go forward
to that from which He has kept them back.

He assigned from His provision to each of their spirits
a nourishment known and apportioned.
No decreaser decreases those whom He increases,
no increaser increases those of them whom He decreases.

Then for each spirit He strikes a fixed term in life,
for each He sets up a determined end;
he walks toward it through the days of his span,
he overtakes it through the years of his time.
Then, when he takes his final step
and embraces the reckoning of his span,
God seizes him to the abundant reward
or the feared punishment
to which He has called him,
That He may repay those who do evil for what they have done
and repay those who do good with goodness,
as justice from Him
(holy are His names, and manifest His boons).

He shall not be questioned as to what He does, but they shall be questioned.

Praise belongs to God, for,
had He withheld from His servants the knowledge to praise Him
for the uninterrupted kindnesses
with which He has tried them and the manifest favors
which He has lavished upon them,
they would have moved about in His kindnesses
without praising Him,
and spread themselves out in His provision
without thanking Him.
Had such been the case,
they would have left the bounds of humanity
for that of beastliness
and become as He has described in the firm text of His Book:
They are but as the cattle -- nay, but they are further astray from the way!

Praise belongs to God, for
the true knowledge of Himself He has given to us,
the thanksgiving He has inspired us to offer Him,
the doors to knowing His Lordship He has opened for us,
the sincerity towards Him in professing His Unity
to which He has led us,
and the deviation and doubt in His Command
from which He has turned us aside;
a praise through

which we may be given long life
among those of His creatures who praise Him,
and overtake those who have gone ahead
toward His good pleasure and pardon;
a praise through which
He will illuminate for us the shadows of the interworld,
ease for us the path of the Resurrection,
and raise up our stations
at the standing places of the Witnesses on the day when
every soul will be repaidfor what it has earned -
they shall not be wronged;

the day a master shall avail nothing a client,
and they shall not be helped;
a praise
which will rise up from us to the highest of the 'Illiyun
in a book inscribed,
witnessed by those brought nigh, a
praise whereby
our eyes may be at rest when sight is dazzled,
our faces whitened when skins are blackened, a
praise through which
we may be released from God's painful Fire
and enter God's generous neighborhood,
a praise by which
we may jostle the angels brought nigh
and join the prophets, the envoys,
in a House of Permanence that does not remove,
the Place of His Generosity that does not change.

Praise belongs to God,
who chose for us the good qualities of creation,
granted us the agreeable things of provision,
and appointed for us excellence
through domination over all creation;
every one of His creatures submits to us
through His power
and comes to obey usthrough His might.

Praise belongs to God,
who locked for us the gate of need
except toward Him.
So how can we praise Him?
When can we thank Him?
Indeed, when?

Praise belongs to God,
who placed within us the organs of expansion,
assigned for us the agents of contraction,
gave us to enjoy the spirits of life,
fixed within us the limbs of works,

nourished us with the agreeable things of provision,
freed us from need through His bounty,
and gave us possessions through His kindness.
Then He commanded us that He might test our obedience
and prohibited us that He might try our thanksgiving.
So we turned against the path of His commandments
and mounted the backs of His warnings.
Yet He hurried us not to His punishment,
nor hastened us on to His vengeance.
No, He went slowly with us through His mercy,
in generosity,
and awaited our return through His clemency,
in mildness.

Praise belongs to God,
who showed us the way to repentance,
which we would not have won save through His bounty.
Had we nothing to count as His bounty but this,
His trial of us would have been good,
His beneficence toward us great,
His bounty upon us immense.
For such was not His wont in repentancewith those who
went before us.
He has lifted up from us
what we have not the strength to bear,
charged us only to our capacity,
imposed upon us nothing but ease,
and left none of us with an argument or excuse.
So the perisher among us is he who perishes in spite of Him
and the felicitous among us he who beseeches Him.

And praise belongs to God
with all the praises of
His angels closest to Him,
His creatures most noble in His eyes,
and His praisers most pleasing to Him;
a praise that may surpass other praises
as our Lord surpasses all His creatures.

Then to Him belongs praise,

in place of His every favor upon us
and upon all His servants, past and still remaining,
to the number of all things His knowledge encompasses,
and in place of each of His favors,
their number doubling and redoubling always and forever,
to the Day of Resurrection;
a praise whose bound has no utmost end,
whose number has no reckoning,
whose limit cannot be reached,
whose period cannot be cut off;
a praise which will become
a link to His obedience and pardon,
a tie to His good pleasure,
a means to His forgiveness,
a path to His Garden,
a protector against His vengeance,
a security against His wrath,
an aid to obeying Him,
a barrier against disobeying Him,
a help in fulfilling His right and His duties;
a praise that will make us felicitous
among His felicitous friends,
and bring us into the ranks
of those martyred by the swords of His enemies.
He is a Friend, Praiseworthy!

S02 - Blessing upon Muhammad and his Household

After this praise of God, he (upon him be peace) would supplicate by calling down blessings upon God's Messenger (God bless him and his Household)

Praise belongs to God
who was kind to us through
Muhammad (God bless him and his Household)
to the exclusion of past communities and bygone generations,
displaying thereby His power,
which nothing can render incapable,
though it be great,
and nothing can escape,
though it be subtle.
He sealed through us all He created,
appointed us witnesses over those who deny,
and increased us by His kindness over those who are few.

O God,
bless Muhammad,
entrusted by You with Your revelation,
distinguished by You among Your creatures,
devoted to You among Your servants,
the imam of mercy,
the leader of good,
the key to blessing,
who wearied his soul
for Your affairs,
exposed his body to detested things
for Your sake,
showed open enmity toward his next of kin
by summoning to You,
fought against his family
for Your good pleasure,
cut the ties of the womb
in giving life to Your religion,
sent far those close
because of their denial,
brought near those far

because of their response to You,
showed friendship to the most distant
for Your sake,
displayed enmity toward the nearest
for Your sake,
made his soul persevere
in delivering Your message,
tired it in summoning
to Your creed,
busied it in counselling
those worthy of Your summons,
migrated to the land of exile and the place of remoteness from
the home of his saddlebags,
the walkway of his feet,
the ground of his birth,
and the intimate abode of his soul,
desiring to exalt Your religion
and seeking help
against those who disbelieved in You,
until what he attempted against Your enemies
went well with him
and what he arranged for Your friends
was accomplished.
He rose up against them seeking victory
through Your aid,
becoming strong in spite of his weakness
with Your help.
He fought against them
in the center of their cities
and attacked them
in the midst of their dwellings,
until Your command prevailed,
and Your word rose up,
though the idolaters were averse.

O God,
so raise him, because of his labors for Your sake,
to the highest degree of Your Garden,
that none may equal him in station,

none may match him in level,
and no angel brought nigh or prophet sent out
may parallel him in Your sight.

And inform him concerning his Household the pure
and his community the faithful
of an excellent intercession,
greater than what You have promised him!

O Keeper of promises!
O Faithful to Your word!
O He who changes evil deeds into manifold good deeds!
You are of bounty abounding!

S03 – Blessing upon the Bearers of the Throne

A supplication in Calling down Blessings upon the Bearers of the Throne and Every Angel Brought Nigh

O God,
as for the Bearers of Your Throne,
who never flag in glorifying You,
never become weary of calling You holy,
never tire of worshipping You,
never prefer curtailment over diligence in Your command,
and are never heedless of passionate love for You;

Seraphiel,
the Owner of the Trumpet,
fixed in his gaze,
awaiting Your permission
and the descent of the Command,
that he may arouse through the Blast
the hostages thrown down in the graves;

Michael,
possessor of standing with You
and a raised up place in Your obedience;

Gabriel,
entrusted with Your revelation,
obeyed by the inhabitants of Your heavens,
distinguished in Your Presence,
brought nigh to You;
the spirit who is over the angels of the veils;
and the spirit
who is of Your command

bless them and the angels below them:
the residents in Your heavens,

those entrusted with Your messages,
those who become not wearied by perseverance,
or exhausted and flagged by toil,
whom passions distract not from glorifying You,
and whose magnification of You is never cut off
by the inattention of heedless moments;
their eyes lowered,
they do not attempt to look at You;
their chins bowed,
they have long desired what is with You;
unrestrained in mentioning Your boons,
they remain humble before Your mightiness
and the majesty of Your magnificence;
those who say when they look upon Gehenna
roaring over the people who disobeyed You:
'Glory be to You,
we have not worshipped You
with the worship You deserve!'

Bless them,
and Your angels who are the Reposeful,
those of proximity to You,
those who carry the unseen to Your messengers,
those entrusted with Your revelation,
the tribes of angels
whom You have singled out for Yourself,
freed from need for food and drink by their calling You holy,
and made to dwell inside Your heavens' layers,
those who will stand upon the heavens' border
when the Command descends to complete Your promise,
the keepers of the rain,
the drivers of the clouds,
him at whose driving's sound is heard the rolling of thunder,
and when the reverberating clouds swim before his driving,
bolts of lightning flash;
the escorts of snow and hail,
the descenders with the drops of rain when they fall,
the watchers over the treasuries of the winds,
those charged with the mountains lest they disappear,

those whom You have taught the weights of the waters
and the measures contained by torrents and masses of rain;
the angels who are Your messengers to the people of the earth
with the disliked affliction that comes down
and the beloved ease;
the devoted, noble scribes,
the watchers, noble writers,
the angel of death and his helpers,
Munkar and Nakir,
Rumaan, the tester in the graves,
the circlers of the Inhabited House,
Malik and the guardians,
Ridwan and the gatekeepers of the gardens,
those who disobey not God in What He commands them
and do What they are commanded;
those who say, Peace be upon you, for that you were patient
and fair is the Ultimate Abode;
the Zabaniya, who, when it is said to them,
take him, and fetter him,
then roast him in hell,
hasten to accomplish it,
nor do they give him any respite;
him whom we have failed to mention,
not knowing his place with You,
nor with which command You have charged him;
and the residents in the air, the earth, and the water,
and those of them charged over the creatures;
bless them on the day when every soul will come,
with it a driver and a witness,
and bless them with a blessing that will add
honor to their honor
and purity to their purity.

O God,
and when You bless Your angels and Your messengers
and You extend our blessings to them,
bless us through the good words about them
which You have opened up for us!
You are Munificent, Generous.

S04 – Blessings upon the Attesters to the Messengers

His Supplication in Calling Down Blessings upon the Followers of and Attesters to the Messengers

O God,
as for the followers of the messengers
and those of the people of the earth
who attested to them unseen
(while the obstinate resisted them through crying lies) -
they yearned for the emissaries through the realities of faith,

in every era and time in which You did send a messenger
and set up for the people a director
from the period of Adam down to Muhammad
(God bless him and his Household)
from among the imams of guidance
and the leaders of the Godfearing
(upon them all be peace) -
remember them with forgiveness and good pleasure!

O God,
and as for the Companions of Muhammad specifically,
those who did well in companionship,
who stood the good test in helping him,
responded to him
when he made them hear his messages' argument,
separated from mates and children
in manifesting his word,
fought against fathers and sons
in strengthening his prophecy,
and through him gained victory;
those who were wrapped in affection for him,
hoping for a commerce
that comes not to naught in love for him;
those who were left by their clans
when they clung to his handhold

and denied by their kinsfolk
when they rested in the shadow of his kinship;

forget not, O God,
what they abandoned for You and in You,
and make them pleased with Your good pleasure
for the sake of the creatures they drove to You
while they were with Your Messenger,
summoners to You for You.

Show gratitude to them for leaving the abodes of their people for Your sake
and going out from a plentiful livelihood to a narrow one,
and [show gratitude to] those of them who became objects of wrongdoing
and whom You multiplied in exalting Your religion.

O God,
and give to those
who have done well in following the Companions,
who say, Our Lord, forgive us and our brothers
who went before us in faith,
Your best reward;
those who went straight to the Companions' road,
sought out their course,
and proceeded in their manner.
No doubt concerning their sure insight diverted them
and no uncertainty shook them
from following in their tracks
and being led by the guidance of their light.
As their assistants and supporters,
they professed their religion,
gained guidance through their guidance,
came to agreement with them,
and never accused them in what they passed on to them.

O God,
and bless the Followers,

from this day of ours to the Day of Doom,
their wives,
their offspring,
and those among them who obey You,
with a blessing through which
You will preserve them from disobeying You,
make room for them in the plots of Your Garden,
defend them from the trickery of Satan,
help them in the piety in which they seek help from You,
protect them from sudden events that come by night and day
- except the events which come with good -
and incite them to
tie firmly the knot of good hope in You,
what is with You,
and refrain from ill thoughts [toward You]
because of what the hands of Your servants' hold.

Thus You may
restore them to beseeching You and fearing You,
induce them to renounce the plenty of the immediate,
make them love to
work for the sake of the deferred
and prepare for what comes after death,
make easy for them every distress that comes to them
on the day when souls take leave from bodies,
release them from
that which brings about the perils of temptation
and being thrown down in the Fire
and staying forever within it,
and take them to security,
the resting place of the Godfearing.

O He the wonders of whose mightiness will never end!
Bless Muhammad and his Household
and prevent us from deviation concerning Your mightiness!

O He the term of whose kingdom will never cease!
Bless Muhammad and his Household
and release our necks from Your vengeance!

O He the treasuries of whose mercy will never be exhausted!
Bless Muhammad and his Household
and appoint for us a portion of Your mercy!

O He whom eyes fall short of seeing!
Bless Muhammad and his Household
and bring us close to Your nearness!

O He before whose greatness all great things are small!
Bless Muhammad and his Household
and give us honor with You!

O He to whom all hidden tidings are manifest!
Bless Muhammad and his Household
and expose us not before You!

O God,
remove our need for the gifts of the givers
through Your gift,
spare us the loneliness of those who break off
through Your joining,
that we may beseech no one
along with Your free giving,
that we may feel lonely at no one's absence
along with Your bounty!

O God,
bless Muhammad and his Household,

scheme for us, not against us,
devise to our benefit, not to our loss,
give the turn to prevail to us, not to others!

O God,
bless Muhammad and his Household,
protect us from Yourself,
safeguard us through Yourself,
guide us to Yourself,
and take us not far from Yourself!
he whom You protect stays safe, he whom You guide
knows,
and he whom You bring near Yourself takes the spoils.

O God,
bless Muhammad and his Household
and spare us the cutting edge of time's turning changes,
the evil of Satan's snares,
and the bitterness of the sovereign's aggression!

O God,
the spared are spared only through the bounty of Your strength,
so bless Muhammad and his Household
and spare us!
The givers give only through the bounty of Your wealth,
so bless Muhammad and his Household
and give to us!
The guided are guided only by the light of Your face,
so bless Muhammad and his Household
and guide us!

O God,
he whom You befriend will not be injured
by the abandonment of the abandoners,
he to whom You give will not be diminished
by the withholding of the withholders,
he whom You guide will not be misled
by the misguidance of the misguiders.

So bless Muhammad and his Household,

defend us from Your servants
through Your might,
free us from need for other than You
through Your support,
and make us travel the path of the Truth
through Your right guidance!

O God,
bless Muhammad and his Household
and put
the soundness of our hearts
into the remembrance of Your mightiness,
the idleness of our bodies
into giving thanks for Your favor,
and the flow of our tongues
into the description of Your kindness!

O God,
bless Muhammad and his Household
and make us one of
Your summoners who summon to You,
Your guiders who direct to You,
and Your special friends whom You have singled out!

O Most Merciful of the merciful!.

S06 - His Supplication in the Morning and Evening

Praise belongs to God,
who created night and day through His strength,
set them apart through His power,
and appointed for each a determined limit and a drawn-out period.
He makes each of the two enter into its companion,
and makes its companion enter into it,
as an ordainment from Him for His servants
in that through which He feeds them
and with which He makes them grow.

He created for them the night,
that they might rest in it
from tiring movements and wearisome exertions
and He made it a garment for them
that they might be clothed in its ease and its sleep,
that it might be for them refreshment and strength,
that they might reach therein pleasure and passion.

He created for them the daytime,
giving sight,
that they might seek within it of His bounty,
find the means to His provision,
and roam freely in His earth,
searching for that through which to attain the immediate in their life in this world
and to achieve the deferred in their life to come.

Through all of this
He sets right their situation,
tries their records,
and watches their state
in the times for obeying Him,
the way stations of His obligations,
and the places of His ordinances,
that He may repay those who do evil with what they have done
and repay those who do good with goodness.

O God,
to You belongs praise for the sky You have split into dawn for us,
giving us to enjoy thereby the brightness of daytime,
showing us sought-after nourishments,
and protecting us from the striking of blights.

In the morning we and all things, every one, rise for You,
the heaven and the earth
and what You have scattered in each,
the still and the moving,
the resident and the journeying,
what towers up in the air and what hides under the ground.

We rise in the morning in Your grasp:
 Your kingdom and authority contain us
and Your will embraces us.
We move about by Your command
and turn this way and that through Your governing.

We own nothing of the affair
except what You have decreed
and nothing of the good
except what You have given.

This is a fresh, new day,
over us a ready witness.
If we do good,
it will take leave from us with praise,
and if we do evil,
it will part from us in blame.

O God,
bless Muhammad and his Household,

provide us with the day's good companionship
and preserve us against parting from it badly
by doing a misdeed or committing a sin,
whether small or great!

Make our good deeds within it plentiful
empty us therein of evil deeds,
and fill what lies between its two sides for us
with praise and thanksgiving,
wages and stores,
bounty and beneficence!

O God,
ease our burden on the Noble Writers,
fill our pages for us with our good deeds,
and degrade us not before them with our evil works!

O God,
appoint for us in each of the day's hours
a share from Your servants,
a portion of giving thanks to You,
and a truthful witness among Your angels!

O God,
bless Muhammad and his Household
and safeguard us from before us and behind us,
from our right hands and our left hands
and from all our directions,
a safeguarding that will preserve from disobeying You,
guide to obeying You,
and be employed for Your love!

O God,
bless Muhammad and his Household
and give us success in this day of ours,

this night of ours,
and in all our days,
to employ the good,
stay away from the evil,
give thanks for favors,
follow the Sunna's norms,
avoid innovations,
enjoin good behavior,
forbid the disapproved,
defend Islam,
diminish falsehood and abase it,
help the truth and exalt it,
guide the misguided,
assist the weak,
and reach out to the troubled!

O God,
bless Muhammad and his Household
and make this the most fortunate day we have known,
the most excellent companion we have accompanied,
and the best time in which we have lingered!

Place us among the most satisfied of all Your creatures
whom night and day have passed by,
the most thankful of them for the favors You have done,
the firmest of them in the laws You have set down in the Shari'a,
and the most unyielding of them toward the prohibited acts against which You have cautioned!

O God,
I call You to witness
- and You are sufficient witness -
and I call Your heaven and Your earth to witness
and Your angels and Your other creatures who inhabit them
in this my day, this my hour,
this my night, and this my resting place,
that I bear witness that You are God,
other than whom there is no god,
Upholding justice,

Equitable in judgment,
Clement to the servants,
Master of the kingdom,
Compassionate to the creatures,
and that Muhammad is Your servant and Your messenger,
Your chosen from among Your creatures.
You did charge him with Your message and he delivered it;
You did command him to counsel his community and he counseled it.

O God,
so bless Muhammad and his Household more than You have blessed any of Your creatures!
Give him for our sake the best You have given any of Your servants,
and repay him on our behalf better and more generously
than You have repaid any of Your prophets on behalf of his community!

You are All-kind with immensity,
the Forgiver of the great,
and You are more merciful
than every possessor of mercy!
So bless Muhammad and his Household,
the good, the pure,
the chosen, the most distinguished!

S07 - His Supplication in Worrisome Tasks

His Supplication when Faced with a Worrisome Task or when Misfortune Descended and at the Time of Distress

O He through whom the knots of detested things are untied!
O He through whom the cutting edge of hardships is blunted!
O He from whom is begged the outlet to the freshness of relief!

Intractable affairs yield to Your power,
means are made ready by Your gentleness,
the decree goes into effect through Your power,
and all things proceed according to Your desire.

By Your desire
they follow Your command without Your word
and by Your will
they obey Your bans without Your prohibition.

You are the supplicated in worries
and the place of flight in misfortunes;
none of them is repelled unless You repel,
none is removed unless You remove.

Upon me has come down,
My Lord,
something whose weight burdens me
and upon me has fallen something whose carrying oppresses me.

Through Your power
You have brought it down upon me
and through Your authority
You have turned it toward me.

23

None can send away what You have brought,
none can deflect what You have turned,
none can open what You have closed,
none can close what You have opened,
none can make easy what You have made difficult,
none can help him whom You have abandoned.

So bless Muhammad and his Household,
open for me,
my Lord,
the door of relief through Your graciousness,
break from me the authority of worry by Your strength,
confer the beauty of Your gaze upon my complaint,
let me taste the sweetness of benefaction in what I ask,
give me from Yourself mercy and wholesome relief,
and appoint for me from Yourself a quick way out!

Distract me not through worry from observing Your obligations
and acting in accordance with Your prescriptions.

My capacity has been straitened,
my Lord,
by what has come down on me,
and I am filled with worry
by carrying what has happened to me,
while You have power to remove what has afflicted me
and to repel that into which I have fallen.

So do that for me
though I merit it not from You,
O Possessor of the Mighty Throne!

His Supplication in Seeking Refuge from Hateful Things, Bad Moral Qualities, and Blameworthy Acts

O God,
I seek refuge in You
from the agitation of craving,
the violence of wrath,
the domination of envy,
the frailty of patience,
the lack of contentment,
surliness of character,
urgency of passion,
the disposition to vehemence,

following caprice,
opposing guidance,
the sleep of heedlessness,
undertaking the toilsome,
preferring falsehood over truth,
persisting in sin,
making little of disobedience,
making much of obedience,

vying with the wealthy,
disparaging the poor,
guarding badly over those in our hands,
failing to thank those who have done good to us,

aiding a wrongdoer,
abandoning someone troubled,
wanting what is not rightfully ours,
and speaking about knowledge without knowing.

We seek refuge in You from harboring dishonesty toward anyone,
being pleased with our works,
and stretching out our expectations.

We seek refuge in You from
ill-mindedness,
looking down on the small,
Satan's gaining mastery over us,
time's afflicting us,
and the sovereign's oppressing us.

We seek refuge in You from acting with prodigality
and not having sufficiency.

We seek refuge in You from the gloating of enemies,
indigent need for equals,
living in hardship,
and dying without readiness.

We seek refuge in You from
the most dreadful remorse,
the greatest affliction,
the most wretched wretchedness,
the evil end to the journey,
the deprivation of reward,
and the advent of punishment.

O God,
bless Muhammad and his Household
and through Your mercy,
give to me refuge from all of that,
and to all the faithful,
both men and women!

O Most Merciful of the merciful!

S09 - His Supplication in Yearning

His Supplication in Yearning to Ask Forgiveness from God

O God,
bless Muhammad and his Household,
make us go to the repentance that You love
and make us leave the persistence that You hate!

O God,
when we halt before two decreases,
in religion or in this world,
let the decrease fall upon that which passes quickly
and relent in that which lasts the longer!

When we set out after two concerns,
one of which makes You pleased with us
and the other of which displeases You,
incline us toward that which makes You pleased
and weaken our strength in that which displeases You!

Leave not our souls alone to choose in that,
for they choose falsehood except in as much as You give
success,and they command to evil except in as much as You
have mercy!

O God,
You created us from frailty,
built us up from feebleness,
and began us from a mean water;
we have no force except through Your strength
and no strength except through Your help.

So confirm us by giving us success,
point us the right way by Your pointing,
blind the eyes of our hearts toward everything opposed to Your love,

and set not in any of our limbs passage to disobeying You!

O God,
bless Muhammad and his Household
and assign the whisperings of our hearts,
the movements of our members,
the glances of our eyes,
and the idioms of our tongues,
to that which makes incumbent Your reward,
lest a good deed slip by us,
through which we might deserve Your repayment,
or an evil deed remain with us,
by which we might merit Your punishment!

S10 - His Supplication in Seeking Asylum with God

O God,
if You will,
You will pardon us through Your bounty
and if You will,
You will chastise us through Your justice.

So make our ways smooth to Your pardon through Your kindness
and grant us sanctuary from Your chastisement through Your forbearance,
for none of us has the endurance for Your justice
and none of us can reach deliverance without Your pardon!

O Richest of the rich!
Here we are, Your servants, before You.
I am the neediest of the needy toward You,
so redress our neediness through Your plenty
and cut us not off from our hopes through Your withholding,
lest You make wretched him who seeks felicity through You
and deprive him who seeks help from Your bounty!

Then to whom would we return after You?
Where would we go from Your gate?
Glory be to You!
We are the distressed,
the response to whom
You have made incumbent,
the people from whom
You have promised to remove the evil

That thing most resembling Your will
and that affair most worthy for You in Your mightiness
is showing mercy to him who asks You for mercy
and helping him who seeks help from You.

So show mercy upon our pleading with You

and free us from need when we throw ourselves before You!

O God,
Satan will gloat over us if we follow him in disobeying You,
so bless Muhammad and his Houschold
and let him not gloat over us
after we have renounced him for You
and beseeched You against him!

S11 - His Supplication for Good Outcomes

O He remembering whom brings honor to those who remember!
O He thanking whom brings triumph to those who give thanks!
O He obeying whom brings deliverance to those who obey!

Bless Muhammad and his Household,
and divert our hearts through remembering You from every act of remembrance,
our tongues through thanking You from every act of thanksgiving,
our limbs through obeying You from every act of obedience!

If You have ordained for us idleness from these occupations,
make it an idleness of safety,
within which no ill consequence visits us
or weariness overtakes us!
Then the writers of evil deeds may depart from us
with a page empty of the mention of our evil deeds,
and the writers of good deeds may turn away from us happy
with the good deeds of ours which they have written.

And when the days of our life have passed by,
the terms of our lifetimes have elapsed,
and Your call,
which must come and be answered,
summons us forth,
then bless Muhammad and his Household
and make the outcome of what the writers of our works
count against us
an accepted repentance,
which afterwards gave us no rest
in a sin that we committed
or an act of disobedience that we performed!

Remove not from us any covering with which You
have covered over the heads of the witnesses on the
day when the records of Your servants are tried!

Verily You are compassionate to him who supplicates
You,
the responder to him who calls upon You!

S12 - His Supplication in Confession

His Supplication in Confession and in Seeking Repentance toward God

O God,
three traits have prevented me from asking You
and one trait has urged me on:

I am prevented by
a command You have commanded
in which I have been slow,
a prohibition You have prohibited
toward which I have hurried,
and a favor through which You have favored
for which I have not given sufficient thanks.

I am urged to ask You
by Your gratuitous bounty upon him who
turns his face toward You
and comes to You with a good opinion,
since all Your beneficence is gratuitous bounty
and every one of Your favors a new beginning!

So here I am, my God,
standing at the gate of Your might,
the standing of the lowly, the surrendered,
asking You in my shame,
the asking of the destitute, the pitiful,

admitting to You that at the time of Your beneficence
I surrendered not save through abstaining from disobedience toward You

and in none of my states was I ever without Your Kindness.

Will it profit me, my God,
to admit to You the evil of what I have earned?
Will it save me from You
to confess the ugliness of what I have done?
Or will You impose upon me in this my station Your displeasure?
Will Your hate hold fast to me in the time of my supplication?

Glory be to You!
I do not despair of You,
for You have opened the door of repentance toward Yourself.
Rather, I say,
the words of a lowly servant,
having wronged himself
and made light of his Lord's inviolability,

and whose sins are dreadful, great,
whose days have parted, fled,
until, when he sees the term of his works expired
and the limit of his lifetime reached
and knows with certainty that he has no escape from You,
no place to flee from You,
he turns his face toward You in repeated turning,
makes his repentance toward You sincere,
stands before You with a pure and purified heart,
then supplicates You with a feeble, quiet voice.

He is bowed before You, bent,
his head lowered, thrown down,
his legs shaking in fear,
his tears flooding his cheeks.
He supplicates You:
O Most Merciful of the merciful!
O Most Merciful of those toward whom
seekers of mercy keep on turning!

O Tenderest of those around whom
run seekers of forgiveness!
O He whose pardon is greater
than His vengeance!
O He whose good pleasure is more abundant
than His anger!

O He who seeks His creatures' praise
with excellent forbearance!
O He who has accustomed His servants
to the acceptance of their repeated turning!
O He who seeks to heal their corruption
through repentance!
O He who is pleased with the easy
of their acts!
O He who recompenses with the much
their little!
O He who has made himself accountable to them
to respond to supplication!
O He who pledged Himself by His gratuitous bounty
to give them excellent repayment!

I am not the most disobedient of those who have disobeyed You
and whom You have forgiven,
nor am I the most blameworthy to offer excuses
which You have accepted,
nor am I the most wrongdoing of those who have repented to You,
and to whom You have returned

I repent to You in this my station,
the repentance of one remorseful over what preceded from him hastily,
apprehensive of what has gathered around him,
pure in shame for that into which he has fallen,
knowing that pardoning great sins is nothing great for You.
overlooking enormous misdeeds is not difficult for You,
putting up with indecent crimes does not trouble You,
and the most beloved of Your servants to You are

he who refrains from arrogance before You
pulls aside from persistence,
and holds fast to praying forgiveness!

I am clear before You of arrogance,
I seek refuge in You from persistence,
I pray forgiveness from You for shortcomings,
I seek help from You in incapacity!

O God,
bless Muhammad and his Household,
dispense with what is incumbent upon me toward You,
release me from what I merit from You,
and grant me sanctuary from what the evildoers fear!
For You are full of pardon,
the hoped-for source of forgiveness,
well known for Your forbearance.
My need has no object but You,
my sin no forgiver other than You –
could that be possible?

I have no fear for myself except from You;
You are worthy of reverential fear,
and worthy to forgive!
Bless Muhammad and his Household,
grant my need,
answer my request favorably,
forgive my sin,
and give me security from fear for myself!
You are powerful over everything,
and that is easy for You.
Amen, Lord of the worlds!

S13 - His Supplication in Seeking Needs from God

O God,
O ultimate object of needs!
O He through whom requests are attained!
O He whose favors are not bought by prices!
O He who does not muddy His gifts
by the imposition of obligations!
O He along with whom nothing is needed
and without whom nothing can be done!
O He toward whom desire is ever directed
and never turned away!
O He whose treasuries cannot be exhausted
by demands!
O He whose wisdom cannot be altered
by any means!
O He from whom the needs of the needy
are never cut off!
O He who is not distressed by the supplications of the supplicators!
You have lauded Yourself for having no need for Your creatures,
and it suits You to have no need for them,
and You have attributed to them poverty,
and it suits them to be poor toward You.

So he who strives to remedy his lack through what is with You
and wishes to turn poverty away from himself through You
has sought his need in the most likely place
and come to his request from the right quarter.

But he who turns in his need toward one of Your creatures
or assigns the cause of its being granted to other than You,
has exposed himself to deprivation
and deserves to miss Your beneficence.

O God,
I have a need of You:
My exertion has fallen short of it

and my stratagems have been cut back before reaching it.
My soul induced me to present it to him who presents his needs to You
and can do nothing without You in his requests,
but this is one of the slips of the offenders,
one of the stumbles of the sinners!

Then through Your reminding me,
I was aroused from my heedlessness,
through Your giving success,
I stood up from my slip,
and through Your pointing the way,
I returned and withdrew from my stumble.

I said:
Glory to my Lord!
How can the needy ask from the needy?
How can the destitute beseech the destitute?

So I went straight to You,
my God,
in beseeching,
and I sent You my hope with trust in You.

I came to know that
the many I request from You are few before Your wealth,
the weighty I ask from You is vile before Your plenty;
Your generosity is not constrained by anyone's asking,
Your hand is higher in bestowing gifts than every hand!

O God,
so bless Muhammad and his Household,
take me through Your generosity
to Your gratuitous bounty
and take me not through Your justice
to what I deserve!

I am not the first beseecher to beseech You
and You bestowed upon him
while he deserved withholding,
nor am I the first to ask from You
and You were bounteous toward him
while he merited deprivation.

O God,
bless Muhammad and his Household,
respond to my supplication,
come near my call,
have mercy on my pleading,
listen to my voice,

cut not short my hope for You,
sever not my thread to You,
turn not my face in this my need,
and other needs,
away from You,

attend for my sake to
the fulfillment of my request,
the granting of my need,
and the attainment of what I have asked
before I leave this place
through Your making easy for me the difficult
and Your excellent ordainment for me in all affairs!

Bless Muhammad and his Household
with a permanent,
ever-growing blessing,
whose perpetuity has no cutting off
and whose term knows no limit,
and make that a help to me
and a cause for the granting of my request!
You are Boundless, Generous!

And of my needs,
My Lord,
are such and such.

HERE YOU SHOULD STATE YOUR NEEDS,
THEN PROSTRATE YOURSELF,
AND SAY IN YOUR PROSTRATION

Your bounty has comforted me
and Your beneficence has shown the way,
So I ask You by You
and by Muhammad and his Household
(Your blessings be upon them)
that You send me not back in disappointment!

S14 - His Supplication in Acts of Wrongdoing

His Supplication when hostility was shown to him or when he saw what he did not like in wrongdoers

O He from whom is not concealed news of the aggrieved!
O He who has no need to be told about them
by the witnessing of the witnesses!
O He who whose help is near to the wronged!
O He whose aid is far from the wrongdoers!

You know, my God,
how so-and-so, son of so-and-so,
has harmed me in that which You have forbidden,
and how he has violated me in that which You have prohibited,
showing thereby ingratitude toward Your favor upon him
and delusion concerning what You have denied him.

O God,
so bless Muhammad and his Household,
keep my wrongdoing enemy from wronging me through Your strength,
blunt his blade toward me through Your power,
and assign to him
a diversion in that which is close to him
and the inability to reach his enemy!

O God,
bless Muhammad and his Household,
let the wrongdoer not find it easy to wrong me,
give me good help against him,
preserve me from the like of his acts,
and place me not in the like of his situation!

O God,
bless Muhammad and his Household,

and assist me with an immediate assistance
that will heal my rage toward him
and redeem my fury toward him!

O God,
bless Muhammad and his Household,
compensate me for his wronging me with Your pardon
and replace his evil action toward me with Your mercy,
for every detested thing less than Your anger is slight
and every disaster next to Your rancor indifferent!

O God,
just as You have made me detest being wronged,
so also protect me from doing wrong!

O God,
I complain to no one but You,
and I seek help from no ruler other than You -
how could I?
So bless Muhammad and his Household,
join my supplication to response,
and unite my complaint with change!

O God,
tempt me not with despair of Your just treatment
and tempt him not with feeling secure from Your disapproval,
lest he persist in wronging me
and constrain me in my rights.
Let him soon recognize
what You have promised the wrongdoers
and let me recognize
Your promised response to the distressed!

O God,
bless Muhammad and his Household,

give me success in accepting Your decrees
for me and against me,
make me pleased with what You take
for me and from me,
guide me to that which is most upright
and employ me in that which is safest!

O God,
if the best for me with You lies
in delaying the taking to task for my sake
of him who has wronged me
and in refraining from vengeance toward him
until the Day of Decision
and the Gathering of Disputants,
then bless Muhammad and his Household,
strengthen me from You
with true intention
and lasting patience,

give me refuge
from evil desire
and the impatience of the greedy,
and form in my heart the image of Your reward
which You have stored away for me
and the repayment and punishment
which You have prepared for my disputant!
Make this a cause of my contentment
with what You have decreed
and my trust
in what You have chosen!

Amen, Lord of the worlds!
You are of bounty abounding
and You are powerful over everything.

S15 - His Supplication when Sick

O God, to You belongs praise
for the good health of my body
which lets me move about,
and to You belongs praise,
for the ailments
which You cause to arise in my flesh!

For I know not, my God,
which of the two states deserves more my thanking You
and which of the two times is more worthy for my praise of You:

the time of health,
within which You make me delight
in the agreeable things of Your provision,
through which You give me the joy to seek
the means to Your good pleasure and bounty,
and by which You strengthen me
for the acts of obedience
which You have given me success to accomplish;

or the time of illness
through which You put me to the test
and bestow upon me favors:
lightening of the offenses
that weigh down my back,
purification of the evil deeds
into which I have plunged,
incitement to reach
for repentance,
reminder of the erasure of misdeeds
through ancient favor;

and, through all that, what the two writers write for me:
blameless acts,

which no heart had thought,
no tongue had uttered,
and no limb had undertaken,
rather, as Your bestowal of bounty upon me
and the beneficence of Your benefaction toward me

O God,
bless Muhammad and his Household,
make me love
what You have approved for me,
make easy for me
what You have sent down upon me,
purify me of the defilement
of what I have sent ahead,
erase the evil
of what I have done beforehand,
let me find the sweetness
of well-being,
let me taste the coolness
of safety,
and appoint for me
a way out from my illness to Your pardon,
transformation of my infirmity into Your forbearance,
escape from my distress to Your refreshment,
and safety from this hardship in Your relief!

You are gratuitously bountiful in beneficence,
ever gracious in kindness,
the Generous, the Giver,
Possessor of majesty and munificence!

S16 - His Supplication in Asking for Release from Sins

O God,
O He through whose Mercy sinners seek aid!
O He to the remembrance of whose beneficence the distressed flee!
O He in fear of whom the offenders weep!
O Comfort of every lonely stranger!
O Relief of all who are downcast and distressed!
O Aid of everyone abandoned and alone!
O Support of every needy outcast!
You are He
who embraces everything in mercy and knowledge!
You are He
who have appointed for each creature a share of Your favors!
You are He
whose pardon is higher than His punishment!
You are He
whose mercy runs before His wrath!
You are He
whose bestowal is greater than His withholding!
You are He
by whose mercy all creatures are embraced!
You are He
who desires no repayment by him upon whom He bestows!
You are He
who does not overdo the punishment of him who disobeys You!

And I, my God, am Your servant
whom You commanded to supplicate
and who said:
I am at Your service and disposal!
Here am I, my Lord,
thrown down before You.
I am he
whose back offenses have weighed down!
I am he
whose lifetime sins have consumed!
I am he
who was disobedient in his ignorance,

while You did not deserve that from him!

Will You, my God,
be merciful toward him who supplicates You,
that I should bring my supplication before You?
Will You forgive him who weeps to You
that I should hurry to weep?
Will You show forbearance toward
him who puts his face in the dust before You in lowliness?
Will You free from need
him who complains to You of his indigent need with confidence?

My God,
disappoint not him who finds no bestower
other than You,
and abandon not him who cannot be freed from his need for You
through less than You!
My God,
so bless Muhammad and his Household,
turn not away from me
when I have turned my face toward You,
deprive me not
when 1 have besought You,
and slap not my brow with rejection
when I have stood before You!
You are He who has described Himself by mercy,
so bless Muhammad and his Household
and have mercy upon me!
You are He who has named Himself by pardon,
so pardon me!

You have seen, my God,
the flow of my tears
in fear of You,
the throbbing of my heart
in dread of You,
and the infirmity of my limbs

in awe of You.
All this from my shame before You
because of my evil works!
So my voice has become silent,
no longer crying to You,
and my tongue has gone dumb,
no longer whispering in prayer.

My God,
so to You belongs praise!
How many of my flaws You have covered over
without exposing me!
How many of my sins You have cloaked
without making me notorious!
How many faults I have committed, yet You did not
tear away from me their covering,
collar me with their detested disgrace,
or make their dishonor plain
to those of my neighbors who search for my defects
and to those who envy Your favor toward me!

But that did not prevent me from passing on
to the evil that You know from me!
So who is more ignorant than I, my God,
of his own right conduct?
Who is more heedless than I
of his own good fortune?
Who is further than I
from seeking to set himself right?

For I spend the provision You deliver to me
in the disobedience You have prohibited to me!
Who sinks more deeply into falsehood
and is more intensely audacious in evil than I?
For I hesitate between Your call and the call of Satan
and then follow his call
without being blind in my knowledge of him

or forgetful in my memory of him,
while I am certain that Your call takes to the Garden
and his call takes to the Fire!

Glory be to You!
How marvelous the witness I bear against my own soul
and the enumeration of my own hidden affairs!
And more marvelous than that is Your lack of haste with me,
Your slowness in attending to me!
That is not because I possess honor with You,
but because You wait patiently for me
and are bountiful toward me
that I may refrain from disobedience displeasing to You
and abstain from evil deeds that disgrace me,
and because You love to pardon me more than to punish!

But I, my God, am
more numerous in sins,
uglier in footsteps,
more repulsive in acts,
more reckless in rushing into falsehood,
weaker in awakening to Your obedience,
and less attentive and heedful toward Your threats,
than that I could number for You my faults
or have the power to recount my sins.

I only scold my own soul,
craving Your gentleness,
through which the affairs of sinners are set right,
and hoping for Your mercy,
through which the necks of the offenders are freed.

O God,
this is my neck,
enslaved by sins,
bless Muhammad and his Household

and release it through Your pardon!
This is my back,
weighed down by offenses,
bless Muhammad and his Household
and lighten it through Your kindness!

My God,
were I to weep to You until my eyelids drop off,
wail until my voice wears out,
stand before You until my feet swell up,
bow to You until my backbone is thrown out of joint,
prostrate to You until my eyeballs fall out,
eat the dirt of the earth for my whole life,
drink the water of ashes till the end of my days,
mention You through all of that until my tongue fails,
and not lift my glance to the sky's horizons in shame before You,
yet would I not merit through all of that
the erasing of a single one of my evil deeds!
Though You forgive me when I merit Your forgiveness
and pardon me when I deserve Your pardon,
yet I have no title to that through what I deserve,
nor am I worthy of it through merit,
since my repayment from You
from the first that I disobeyed You
is the Fire!

So if You punish me,
You do me no wrong.
My God, since You have
shielded me with Your covering
and not exposed me,
waited patiently for me through Your generosity,
and not hurried me to punishment,
and shown me clemency through Your bounty,
and not changed Your favor upon me
or muddied Your kindly acts toward me,
have mercy on my drawn out pleading,
my intense misery,

and my evil situation!

O God,
bless Muhammad and his Household,
protect me from acts of disobedience,
employ me in obedience,
provide me with excellent turning back [to You],
purify me through repentance,
strengthen me through preservation from sin,
set me right through well-being,
let me taste the sweetness of forgiveness,
make me the freedman of Your pardon
and the slave released by Your mercy,
and write for me a security
from Your displeasure!

Give me the good news of that
in the immediate, not the deferred
- a good news I recognize -
and make known to me therein a sign
which I may clearly see!

That will not constrain You in Your plenty,
distress You in Your power,
ascend beyond Your lack of haste,
or tire You in Your great gifts,
which are pointed to by Your signs.

Verily You do what You will,
You decree what You desire.
You are powerful over everything.

O God,
we seek refuge in You
from the instigations of the accursed Satan,
his trickery, and his traps,
from trust in his false hopes, his promises,
his delusions, and his snares,
and lest he should make himself crave
to lead us away from Your obedience
and to degrade us through our disobeying You,
and lest what he has shown us as beautiful be beautiful for us
and what he has shown us as detestable weigh down upon us.

O God,
drive him away from us through Your worship,
throw him down through our perseverance in Your love,
and place between him and us a covering
that he cannot tear away
and a solid barrier
that he cannot cut through!

O God,
bless Muhammad and his Household,
distract Satan from us with some of Your enemies,
preserve us from him through Your good guarding,
spare us his treachery,
turn his back toward us,
and cut off from us his trace!

O God,
bless Muhammad and his Household,
give us to enjoy guidance
the like of his misguidance,
increase us in piety
against his seduction,

and make us walk in reverential fear
contrary to his path of ruin!

O God,
assign him no place of entrance into our hearts
and do not allow him to make his home in that which is with us!

O God,
cause us to recognize the falsehood with which he tempts us,
and once You have caused us to recognize it,
protect us from it!
Make us see what will allow us to outwit him,
inspire us with all that we can make ready for him,
awaken us from the heedless slumber of relying upon him,
and help us well, through Your giving success, against him!

O God,
saturate our hearts with the rejection of his works
and be gentle to us by destroying his stratagems!

O God,
bless Muhammad and his Household,
turn his authority away from us,
cut off his hope from us,
and keep him from craving for us!

O God,
bless Muhammad and his Household,
and place our fathers, our mothers,
our children, our wives,
our siblings, our relatives,
and the faithful among our neighbors,
male and female,
in a sanctuary impregnable to him,
a guarding fortress,

a defending cave!
Clothe them in shields protective against him
and give them arms that will cut him down!

O God,
include in that everyone who
witnesses to You as Lord,
devotes himself sincerely to Your Unity,
shows enmity toward him
through the reality of servanthood,
and seeks help from You against him
through knowledge of the divine sciences!

O God,
undo what he ties,
unstitch what he sews up,
dislocate what he devises,
frustrate him when he makes up his mind,
and destroy what he establishes!

O God,
rout his troops,
nullify his trickery,
make his cave collapse,
and rub his nose in the ground!

O God,
place us in the ranks of his enemies
and remove us from the number of his friends,
that we obey him not when he entices us
and answer him not when he calls to us!
We command everyone who obeys our command
to be his enemy
and we admonish everyone who follows our prohibition
not to follow him!

O God,
bless Muhammad,
the Seal of the prophets and lord of the emissaries,
and the folk of his house,
the good, the pure!
Give refuge to us, our families, our brothers,
and all the faithful, male and female,
from that from which we seek refuge,
and grant us sanctuary from that through fear of which
we seek sanctuary in You!
Hear our supplication to You,
bestow upon us that of which we have been heedless,
and safeguard for us what we have forgotten!
Through all this bring us into the ranks of the righteous
and the degrees of the faithful!
Amen, Lord of the worlds!

S18 - His Supplication in Perils

O God,
to You belongs praise for Your excellent accomplishment
and for Your trial which You have turned away from me!
But make not my share of Your mercy
the well-being which You have quickly granted to me,
lest I become wretched through what I have loved
and someone else gain felicity through what I have disliked!
If this well-being in which 1 pass the day or night should precede a trial that does not cease
and a burden that does not pass away,
then set before me what You had set behind
and set behind me what You had set before!
For that which ends in annihilation is not great
and that which ends in subsistence is not little.
And bless Muhammad and his Household!

S19 - His Supplication in Asking for Water during a Drought

O God,
water us with rain,
unfold upon us Your mercy
through Your copious rain
from the driven clouds,
so that Your goodly earth may grow
on all horizons!

Show kindness to Your servants
through the ripening of the fruit,
revive Your land
through the blossoming of the flowers,
and let Your angels - the noble scribes - be witness
to a beneficial watering from You,
lasting in its abundance,
plenty in its flow,
heavy, quick, soon,

through which You revive what has vanished,
bring forth what is coming,
and provide plentiful foods,
through heaped up, wholesome, productive clouds,
in reverberating layers,
the rain's downpour
not without cease,
the lightning's flashes
not without fruit!

O God,
give us water through rain,
helping, productive, fertilizing,
widespread, plentiful, abundant,
bringing back the risen,
restoring the broken!

O God,
give us water with a watering through which You will
make the stone hills pour,
fill the cisterns,
flood the rivers,
make the trees grow,
bring down prices in all the lands,
invigorate the beasts and the creatures,
perfect for us the agreeable things of provision,
make grow for us the fields,
let flow for us the teats,
and add for us strength to our strength!

O God,
make not the cloud's shadow over us a burning wind,
allow not its coldness to be cutting,
let not its pouring down upon us be a stoning,
and make not its waters for us bitter!

O God,
bless Muhammad and his Household
and provide us with the blessings of the heavens and the earth!
You are powerful over everything

S20 - His Supplication on Noble Moral Traits (Makarimul Akhlaq) Acts Pleasing to God

O God,
bless Muhammad and his Household,
cause my faith to reach the most perfect faith,
make my certainty the most excellent certainty,
and take my intention to the best of intentions
and my works to the best of works!

O God,
complete my intention through Your gentleness,
rectify my certainty through what is with You,
and set right what is corrupt in me through Your power!

O God,
bless Muhammad and his Household,
spare me the concerns which distract me,
employ me in that about which You will ask me tomorrow,
and let me pass my days in that for which You have created me!
Free me from need,
expand Your provision toward me,
and tempt me not with ingratitude!
Exalt me and afflict me not with pride!
Make me worship You and corrupt not my worship with self-admiration!
Let good flow out from my hands upon the people
and efface it not by my making them feel obliged!
Give me the highest moral traits and preserve me from vain glory!

O God,
bless Muhammad and his Household,
raise me not a single degree before the people
without lowering me its like in myself
and bring about no outward exaltation for me
without an inward abasement in myself to the same measure!

O God,
bless Muhammad and Muhammad's Household,
give me to enjoy a sound guidance which I seek not to replace,
a path of truth from which I swerve not,
and an intention of right conduct in which I have no doubts!
Let me live as long as my life is a free gift in obeying You,
but if my life should become a pasture for Satan,
seize me to Yourself before Your hatred overtakes me
or Your wrath against be becomes firm!

O God,
deposit in me no quality for which I will be faulted,
unless You set it right,
no flaw for which I will be blamed,
unless You make it beautiful,
no deficient noble trait,
unless You complete it!

O God,
bless Muhammad and Muhammad's Household
and replace for me the animosity of the people of hatred with love,
the envy of the people of insolence with affection,
the suspicion of the people of righteousness with trust,
the enmity of those close with friendship,
the disrespect of womb relatives with devotion,
the abandonment of relatives with help,
the attachment of flatterers with love set right,
the rejection of fellows with generous friendliness,
and the bitterness of the fear of wrongdoers with the sweetness of security!

O God,
bless Muhammad and his Household,
appoint for me a hand against him who wrongs me,
a tongue against him who disputes with me,
and a victory over him who stubbornly resists me!
Give me guile against him who schemes against me,
power over him who oppresses me,
refutation of him who reviles me,
and safety from him who threatens me!
Grant me success to obey him who points me straight
and follow him who guides me right!

O God,
bless Muhammad and his Household
and point me straight to resist him who is dishonest toward me with good counsel,
repay him who separates from me with gentle devotion,
reward him who deprives me with free giving,
recompense him who cuts me off with joining,
oppose him who slanders me with excellent mention,
give thanks for good,
and shut my eyes to evil!

O God,
bless Muhammad and his Household,
adorn me with the adornment of the righteous,
and clothe me in the ornaments of the Godfearing,
through spreading justice,
restraining rage,
quenching the flame of hate,
bringing together the people of separation,
correcting discord,
spreading about good behavior,
covering faults, mildness of temper,
lowering the wing,
beauty of conduct, gravity of bearing,

agreeableness in comportment,
precedence in reaching excellence,
preferring bounteousness,
refraining from condemnation,
bestowing bounty on the undeserving,
speaking the truth,
though it be painful,
making little of the good in my words and deeds,
though it be much,
and making much of the evil in my words and deeds,
though it be little!
Perfect this for me through lasting obedience,
holding fast to the community,
and rejecting the people of innovation
and those who act in accordance with original opinions!

O God,
bless Muhammad and his Household,
appoint for me Your widest provision in my old age
and Your strongest strength when I am exhausted,
try me not with laziness in worship of You,
blindness toward Your path,
undertaking what opposes love for You,
joining with him who has separated himself from You,
and separating from him who has joined himself to You!

O God,
make me leap to You in times of distress,
ask from You in needs,
and plead to You in misery!
Tempt me not to seek help from other than You when I am distressed,
to humble myself in asking from someone else when I am poor,
or to plead with someone less than You when I fear,
for then I would deserve Your abandonment,
Your withholding,
and Your turning away,
O Most Merciful of the merciful!

O God,
make the wishing, the doubt, and the envy
which Satan throws into my heart
a remembrance of Your mightiness,
a reflection upon Your power,
and a devising against Your enemy!
Make everything he causes to pass over my tongue –
the indecent or ugly words,
the maligning of good repute,
the false witness,
the speaking ill of an absent man of faith
or the reviling of one present,
and all things similar –
a speech in praise of You,
a pursual of eulogizing You,
an excursion in magnifying You,
a thanksgiving for Your favor,
an acknowledgement of Your beneficence,
and an enumeration of Your kindnesses!

O God,
bless Muhammad and his Household,
let me not be wronged while You can repel from me,
let me not do wrong while You are powerful over holding me back,
let me not be misguided while You are able to guide me,
let me not be poor while with You is my plenty,
let me not be insolent while from You comes my wealth!

O God,
I come to Your forgiveness,
I go straight to Your pardon,
I yearn for Your forbearance,
and I trust in Your bounty,
but there is nothing with me to make me warrant Your forgiveness,
nothing in my works to make me merit Your pardon,
and nothing on my behalf after I judge my soul but Your bounty,
so bless Muhammad and his Household

and bestow Your bounty upon me!

O God,
make my speech be guidance,
inspire me with reverential fear,
give me success in that which is most pure,
and employ me in what is most pleasing to You!
O God,
let me tread the most exemplary path
and make me live and die in Your creed!
O God,
bless Muhammad and his Household,
give me to enjoy moderation,
make me into one of the people of right behavior,
the proofs of right conduct,
and the servants of righteousness,
and provide me with triumph at the place of Return
and safety from the Ambush!

O God,
take to Yourself from my soul what will purify it
and leave for my soul that of my soul that will set it right,
for my soul will perish unless You preserve it!

O God,
You are my stores when I sorrow,
You are my recourse when I am deprived,
from You I seek aid when troubled
and with You is a substitute for everything gone by,
a correction for everything corrupted,
and a change from everything You disapprove.
So show kindness to me
with well-being before affliction,
wealth before asking,
right conduct before misguidance;
suffice me against the burden of shame toward the servants,
give me security on the Day of Return,

and grant me excellent right guidance!

O God,
bless Muhammad and his Household,
repel from me through Your gentleness,
feed me through Your favor,
set me right through Your generosity,
heal me through Your benefaction,
shade me in Your shelter,
wrap me in Your good pleasure,
and give me success to reach the most guided of affairs when affairs confuse me,
the purest of works when works seem similar,
and the most pleasing to You of creeds when creeds conflict!

O God,
bless Muhammad and his Household,
crown me with sufficiency,
place in me excellent guardianship,
give me to guide correctly,
tempt me not with plenty,
grant me excellent ease,
make not my life toil and trouble,
and refuse not my supplication in rejection,
for I make none rival to You
and I supplicate none with You as equal!

O God,
bless Muhammad and his Household,
hold me back from prodigality,
fortify my provision against ruin,
increase my possessions through blessing them,
and set me upon the path of guidance through piety in what I spend!

O God,
bless Muhammad and his Household,
spare me the burden of earning,

and provide for me without reckoning,
lest I be distracted from Your worship through seeking
and carry the load of earning's ill results!

O God,
bestow upon me what I seek
through Your power
and grant me sanctuary from what I fear
through Your might!

O God,
bless Muhammad and his Household,
save my face through ease,
and demean not my dignity through neediness,
lest I seek provision from those whom You have provided
and ask for bestowal from the worst of Your creatures!
Then I would be tried by praising him who gave to me
and afflicted with blaming him who held back from me,
while You - not they - are patron of giving and holding back.

O God,
bless Muhammad and his Household
and provide me with soundness in worship,
detachment in renunciation,
knowledge put into action,
and abstinence in measure!

O God,
seal my term with Your pardon,
verify my expectation in hoping for Your mercy,
smooth my paths to reach Your good pleasure,
and make my works good in all my states!

O God,
bless Muhammad and his Household,

incite me to remember You in times of heedlessness,
employ me in Your obedience in days of disregard,
open a smooth road for me to Your love,
and complete for me thereby the good of this world and the next!

O God,
and bless Muhammad and his Household
the best You have blessed any of Your creatures before him
and will bless any of them after him,
and give to us in this World good,
and in the next world good,
and protect me through Your mercy from the chastisement of the Fire!

S21 - His Supplication in Sorrow

His Supplication when Something Made him Sorrow and Offenses Made him Worry

O God,
O Sufficer of the isolated and weak
and Protector against terrifying affairs!
Offenses have isolated me,
so there is none to be my companion.
I am too weak for Your wrath
and there is none to strengthen me.
I have approached the terror of meeting You
and there is none to still my fear.

Who can make me secure from You
when You have filled me with terror?
Who can come to my aid
when You have isolated me?
Who can strengthen me
when You have weakened me?

None can grant sanctuary to a vassal, my God,
but a lord,
none can give security to one dominated
but a dominator,
none can aid him from whom demands are made
but a demander.

In Your hand, my God,
is the thread of all that,
in You the place of escape and flight,
so bless Muhammad and his Household,
give sanctuary to me in my flight,
and grant my request!

O God,
if You should turn Your generous face away from me,
withhold from me Your immense bounty,
forbid me Your provision,
or cut off from me Your thread,
I will find no way to anything of my hope
other than You
nor be given power over what is with You
through another's aid,
for I am Your servant and in Your grasp;
my forelock is in Your hand.

I have no command along with Your command.
'Accomplished is Your judgement of me,
just Your decree for me!
I have not the strength to emerge from Your authority
nor am I able to step outside Your power.
I cannot win Your inclination,
arrive at Your good pleasure,
or attain what is with You
except through obeying You
and through the bounty of Your mercy.

O God,
I rise in the morning and enter into evening
as Your lowly slave.
I own no profit and loss for myself
except through You.
I witness to that over myself
and I confess to the frailty of my strength
and the paucity of my stratagems.
So accomplish what You have promised me
and complete for me what You have given me,
for I am Your slave,
miserable, abased, frail,
distressed, vile, despised,
poor, fearful,
and seeking sanctuary!

O God,
bless Muhammad and his Household
and let me not forget to remember You
in what You have done for me,
be heedless of Your beneficence
in Your trying me,
or despair of Your response to me,
though it keep me waiting,
whether I be in prosperity or adversity,
hardship or ease,
well-being or affliction,
misery or comfort,
wealth or distress,
poverty or riches!

O God,
bless Muhammad and his Household,
make me laud You,
extol You,
and praise You in all my states
so that I rejoice not over
what You give me of this world
nor sorrow over that of it
which You withhold from me!
Impart reverential fear of You to my heart,
employ my body in that which You accept from me,
and divert my soul through obedience to You
from all that enters upon me,
so that I love nothing that displeases You
and become displeased at nothing that pleases You!

O God,
bless Muhammad and his Household,
empty my heart for Your love,
occupy it with remembering You,
animate it with fear of You and quaking before You,

strengthen it with beseeching You,
incline it to Your obedience,
set it running in the path most beloved to You,
and subdue it through desire for what is with You
all the days of my life!

Let my provision in this world
be reverential fear of You,
my journey be toward Your mercy,
and my entrance be into Your good pleasure!
Appoint for me a lodging in Your Garden,
give me strength to bear
everything that pleases You,
make me flee to You
and desire what is with You,
clothe my heart in estrangement
from the evil among Your creatures,
and give me intimacy with You,
Your friends, and those who obey You!

Assign to no wicked person or unbeliever
a kindness toward me
or a hand that obliges me,
nor to me a need for one of them!
Rather make the stillness of my heart,
the comfort of my soul,
my independence and my sufficiency
lie in You and the best of Your creatures!

O God,
bless Muhammad and his Household,
make me their comrade,
make me their helper,
and oblige me with yearning for You
and doing for You what You love and approve!
You are powerful over everything
and that is easy for You.

S22 - His Supplication in Hardship

His Supplication in Hardship, Effort, and Difficult Affairs

O God,
You have charged me concerning myself
with that which belongs more to You than to me.
Your power over it and over me is greater than my power,
so give me in myself
what will make You pleased with me
and take for Yourself
Your good pleasure in my self's well-being!

O God,
I have no endurance for effort,
no patience in affliction,
no strength to bear poverty.
So forbid me not my provision
and entrust me not to Your creatures,
but take care of my need alone
and Yourself attend to sufficing me!

Look upon me and look after me in all my affairs,
for if You entrust me to myself,
I will be incapable before myself
and fail to undertake that in which my best interest lies.
If You entrust me to Your creatures,
they will frown upon me,
and if You make me resort to my kinsfolk,
they will refuse to give to me;
if they give, they will give little and in bad temper,
making me feel long obliged
and blaming me much.

So through Your bounty, O God,
free me from need,
through Your mightiness, lift me up,

through Your boundless plenty, open my hand,
and with that which is with You, suffice me!

O God,
bless Muhammad and his Household,
rid me of envy, encircle me against sins,
make me abstain from things unlawful,
give me not the boldness of disobedient acts,
assign me love for that which is with You
and satisfaction with that which comes to me from You,
bless me in that which You provide me,
that which You confer upon me,
and that through which You favor me,
and make me in all my states
safeguarded, watched, covered, defended,
given refuge, and granted sanctuary!

O God,
bless Muhammad and his Household
and let me accomplish everything
which You have enjoined upon me
or made obligatory for me toward You,
in one of the ways of Your obedience,
or toward one of Your creatures,
though my body be too frail for that,
my strength too feeble,
my power not able to reach it,
and my possessions and what my hand owns
not encompass it,
and whether I have remembered it or forgotten it.

It, my Lord, is among that which
You have counted against me
while I have been heedless of it in myself.
Let me perform it through Your plentiful giving
and the abundance which is with You –
for You are Boundless, Generous –

so that nothing of it may remain against me,
lest You would wish to settle accounts for it
from my good deeds
or to compound my evil deeds
on the day I meet You, my Lord!

O God,
bless Muhammad and his Household
and provide me with desire to serve You
for the sake of my state in the hereafter,
such that I know the truthfulness of that [desire] in my heart,
be dominated by renunciation while in this world,
do good deeds with yearning,
and remain secure from evil deeds in fright and fear!
And give me a light whereby
I may walk among the people,
be guided in the shadows,
and seek illumination in doubt and uncertainty!

O God,
bless Muhammad and his Household
and provide me with fear of the threatened gloom
and yearning for the promised reward,
such that I may find
the pleasure of that for which I supplicate You
and the sorrow of that from which I seek sanctuary in You!

O God,
You know what will set my affairs right
in this world and the next,
so be ever gracious toward my needs!

O God,
bless Muhammad and Muhammad's Household
and provide me with what is Your right
when I fall short in thanking You

for that through which You have favored me
in ease and difficulty,
health and sickness,
such that I may come to know in myself
repose in satisfaction
and serenity of soul
in that which You have made incumbent upon me
in whatever states may occur:
fear and security,
satisfaction and displeasure,
loss and gain!

O God,
bless Muhammad and his Household
and provide me with a breast safe from envy,
such that I envy none of Your creatures
and in anything of Your bounty
and such that I see none of Your favors
toward any of Your creatures
in religion or this world,
well-being or reverential fear,
plenty or ease,
without hoping for myself better than it
through and from You alone,
who has no associate!

O God,
bless Muhammad and his Household
and provide me in this world and the next
with caution against offenses
and wariness against slips
in the state of satisfaction and wrath,
such that I may remain indifferent
toward that which enters upon me
from the two states,
work toward Your obedience,
and prefer it and Your good pleasure over all else
in both friends and enemies.

Then my enemy may stay secure
from my wrongdoing and injustice
and my friend may despair
of my inclination
and the bent of my affection.

Make me one of those who supplicate You
with sincerity in ease
with the supplication of those
who supplicate You with sincerity in distress!
Verily You are Praiseworthy, Glorious.

S23 - His Supplication for Well-Being

His Supplication when he Asked God for Well-Being and Thanked Him for it

O God,
bless Muhammad and his Household,
clothe me in Your well-being,
wrap me in Your well-being,
fortify me through Your well-being,
honor me with Your well-being,
free me from need through Your well-being,
donate to me Your well-being,
bestow upon me Your well-being,
spread out for me Your well-being,
set Your well-being right for me,
and separate me not from Your well-being
in this world and the next!

O God,
bless Muhammad and his Household
and make me well with
a well-being sufficient,
healing, sublime, growing,
a well-being that will give birth to well-being in my body,
a well-being in this world and the next!

Oblige me through
health, security,
and safety in my religion and body,
insight in my heart,
penetration in my affairs,
dread of You,
fear of You,
strength for the obedience
which You have commanded for me,
and avoidance of the disobedience
which You have prohibited for me!

O God,
oblige me through
the hajj, the umrah,
and visiting the graves of Your Messenger
(Your blessings, mercy, and benedictions upon him
and upon his Household)
and the Household of Your Messenger
(upon them be peace)
for as long as You cause me to live,
in this year of mine and in every year,
and make that accepted, thanked,
and mentioned before You
and stored away with You!

Make my tongue utter Your praise,
Your thanksgiving,
Your remembrance,
and Your excellent laudation,
and expand my heart
toward the right goals of Your religion!

Give me and my progeny refuge from
the accursed Satan,
the evil of venomous vermin,
threatening pests,
swarming crowds,
and evil eyes,
the evil of every rebel satan,
the evil of every refractory sovereign,
the evil of everyone living in ease and served,
the evil of everyone weak or strong,
the evil of everyone born high or low,
the evil of everyone small or great,
the evil of everyone near or far,
the evil of everyone, jinn or man,
who declares war on Your Messenger and his Household,
and the evil of every crawling creature

that You have taken by the forelock!
Surely You are on a straight path.

O God,
bless Muhammad and his Household
and if someone desires ill for me
turn him away from me,
drive away from me his deception,
avert from me his evil,
send his trickery back to his own throat,
and place before him a barricade,
so that You may
blind his eyes toward me,
deafen his ears toward my mention,
lock his heart toward recalling me,
silence his tongue against me,
restrain his head,
abase his exaltation,
break his arrogance,
abase his neck,
disjoint his pride,
and make me secure from all his injury,
his evil, his slander,
his backbiting, his faultfinding,
his envy, his enmity,
his snares, his traps,
his foot soldiers, and his cavalry!
Surely You are Mighty, Powerful!

S24 - His Supplication for his Parents (upon the two of them be peace)

O God,
bless Muhammad, Your slave and Your messenger,
and his Household, the pure,
and single them out for the best of Your blessings,
Your mercy,
Your benedictions,
and Your peace!

And single out my parents, O God,
for honor with You and blessings from You,
O Most Merciful of the merciful!

O God,
bless Muhammad and his Household,
teach me through inspiration
knowledge of everything incumbent upon me toward them,
and gather within me
knowledge of all that completely!
Then make me act in accordance
with what You have inspired me
and give me the success to put into practice
the knowledge You have shown to me,
lest I fail to act
according to something You have taught me
or my limbs feel too heavy to perform
that with which You have inspired me!

O God,
bless Muhammad and his Household,
as You have ennobled us through him,
and bless Muhammad and his Household,
as You have made incumbent upon us
rights toward the creatures because of him!

O God,
fill me with awe of my parents,
the awe one has toward a tyrannical sovereign,
and let me be devoted to them,
with the devotion of a compassionate mother!
Make my obedience and devotion to them
more gladdening to my eyes
than sleep to the drowsy
and more refreshing to my breast
than drink to the thirsty,
so that I may prefer their inclination
to my inclination,
set their satisfaction
before my satisfaction,
make much of their devotion to me
though it be little,
and make little of my devotion to them
though it be great.

O God,
lower before them my voice,
make agreeable to them my words,
make mild before them my temper,
make tender toward them my heart,
and turn me into their kind companion,
their loving friend!

O God,
thank them for my upbringing,
reward them for honoring me,
and guard them as they guarded me in my infancy!

O God,
and whatever harm has touched them from me,
detested thing has reached them from me,
or right of theirs which has been neglected by me,
allow it to alleviate their sins,

raise them in their degrees,
and add to their good deeds!
O He who changes evil deeds into manifold good deeds!

O God,
whatever word through which they have transgressed against me,
act through which they have been immoderate with me,
right of mine which they have left neglected,
or obligation toward me in which they have fallen short,
I grant it to them
and bestow it upon them,
and I beseech You
to remove from them its ill consequence,
for I do not accuse them concerning myself,
find them slow in their devotion toward me,
or dislike the way they have attended to my affairs, my Lord!

They have rights against me which are more incumbent,
precedence in beneficence toward me that is greater,
and kindness toward me that is mightier
than that I should settle accounts with justice
or repay them with equivalents.
Where then, my God, would be their long occupation
with bringing me up?
Where the hardship of their toil
in taking care of me?
Where the stinting of themselves
to provide me with plenty?

What an idea!
I can never discharge their right against me,
fulfil my obligations toward them,
or accomplish the duty of serving them.
So bless Muhammad and his Household
and help me, O Best of those whose help we seek!
Give me success,
O Most Guiding of those whom we beseech!

Place me not among the people of disrespect to fathers and mothers
on the day when every soul will be repaid
for what it has earned,
they shall not be wronged.
O God,
bless Muhammad, his Household, and his progeny
and single out my parents for the best
which You have singled out
for the fathers and mothers of Your faithful servants,
O Most Merciful of the merciful!

O God,
let me not forget to remember them after my ritual prayers,
at every time throughout my night,
and in each of the hours of my day!

O God,
bless Muhammad and his Household,
forgive me through my supplication for my parents,
forgive them through their devotion toward me
with unfailing forgiveness,
be well pleased with them through my intercession for them
with resolute good pleasure,
and make them reach through Your generosity
the abodes of safety!

O God,
if Your forgiveness reaches them first,
make them my intercessors,
and if Your forgiveness reaches me first,
make me their intercessors,
so that we may gather together through Your gentleness
in the house of Your generosity
and the place of Your forgiveness and mercy!
Verily You are Possessor of abounding bounty
and ancient kindness,
and You are the Most Merciful of the merciful!

S25 - His Supplication for his Children

O God,
be kind to me through
the survival of my children,
setting them right for me,
and allowing me to enjoy them!

My God,
make long their lives for me,
increase their terms,
bring up the smallest for me,
strengthen the weakest for me,
rectify for me
their bodies,
their religious dedication,
and their moral traits,
make them well in
their souls,
their limbs,
and everything that concerns me of their affair,
and pour out for me and upon my hand
their provisions!

Make them
pious, fearing,
insightful, hearing,
and obedient toward You,
loving and well-disposed
toward Your friends,
and stubbornly resistant and full of hate
toward all Your enemies!
Amen!

O God,
through them

strengthen my arm,
straighten my burdened back,
multiply my number,
adorn my presence,
keep alive my mention,
suffice me when I am away,
help me in my needs,
and make them
loving toward me,
affectionate, approaching,
upright, obedient,
never disobedient, disrespectful,
opposed, or offenders!

Help me in their upbringing,
their education,
and my devotion toward them,
give me among them from Yourself male children,
make that a good for me,
and make them a help for me
in that which I ask from You!

Give me and my progeny refuge from the accursed Satan,
for You have created us,
commanded us,
and prohibited us,
and made us
desire the reward of what You have commanded,
and fear its punishment!
You assigned to us an enemy
who schemes against us,
gave him an authority over us
in a way that You did not give us authority over him,
allowed him to dwell in our breasts
and let him run in our blood vessels;
he is not heedless,
though we be heedless,
he does not forget,

though we forget;
he makes us feel secure from Your punishment
and fills us with fear toward other than You.

If we are about to commit an indecency,
he gives us courage to do so,
and if we are about to perform a righteous work,
he holds us back from it.
He opposes us through passions,
and sets up for us doubts.
If he promises us, he lies,
and if he raises our hopes, he fails to fulfil them.
If You do not turn his trickery away from us,
he will misguide us,
and if You do not protect us from his corruption,
he will cause us to slip.

O God,
so defeat his authority over us through Your authority,
such that You hold him back from us
through the frequency of our supplication to You
and we leave his trickery
and rise up among those preserved by You from sin!

O God,
grant me my every request,
accomplish for me my needs,
withhold not from me Your response
when You have made Yourself accountable for it to me,
veil not my supplication from Yourself,
when You have commanded me to make it,
and be kind to me through everything that will set me right
in this world and the next,
in everything that I remember or forget,
display or conceal,
make public or keep secret!

In all of this, place me through my asking You among
those who set things right,
those who are answered favorably
when they request from You
and from whom is not withheld
when they put their trust in You,
those accustomed to seek refuge in You,
those who profit through commerce with You,
those granted sanctuary
through Your might,
those given lawful provision in plenty from Your boundless bounty
through Your munificence and generosity,
those who reach exaltation after abasement
through You,
those granted sanctuary from wrong
through Your justice,
those released from affliction
through Your mercy,
those delivered from need after poverty
through Your riches,
those preserved from sins, slips, and offenses
through reverential fear toward You,
those successful in goodness, right conduct, and propriety
through obeying You,
those walled off from sins
through Your power,
the refrainers from every act of disobedience toward You,
the dwellers in Your neighborhood!

O God,
give me all of that through Your bestowal of success and Your mercy,
grant us refuge from the chastisement of the burning,
and give to
all the Muslims, male and female,
and all the faithful, male and female,
the like of what I have asked for myself and my children,
in the immediate of this world
and the deferred of the next!

Verily You are the Near, the Responder,
the All-hearing, the All-knowing,
the Pardoner, the Forgiving,
the Clement, the Merciful!

And give to us in this world good,
and in the next world good,
and protect us from the chastisement of the Fire

S26 - His Supplication for his Neighbors and Friends

O God,
bless Muhammad and his Household and
attend to me with Your best attending in
my neighbors and friends who recognize
our right
and war against our enemies!

Give [my neighbors and friends] success in
performing Your prescriptions
and taking on the beauties of Your courtesy through
acting gently with their weak,
remedying their lacks,
visiting their sick,
guiding their seeker of right guidance,
giving good counsel to their seeker of advice,
attending to the one among them who returns from travel,
hiding their secrets,
covering over their shameful things,
helping their wronged,
sharing kindly with them in goods,
turning toward them with wealth and bestowal of bounty,
and giving what is due to them before they ask!

Let me, O God,
repay their evildoer
with good-doing,
turn away from their wrongdoer
with forbearance.
have a good opinion
of every one of them,
attend to all of them
with devotion,
lower my eyes before them
in continence,
make mild my side toward them
in humility,

be tender toward the afflicted among them
in mercy,
make them happy in absence
through affection,
love that they continue to receive favor
through good will,
grant them
what I grant my next of kin,
and observe for them
what I observe for my special friends!

O God,
bless Muhammad and his Household,
provide me the like of that from them,
appoint for me the fullest share of what is with them,
increase them
in insight toward my right
and knowledge of my excellence
so that they will be fortunate through me
and I fortunate through them!
Amen, Lord of the worlds!

S27 - His Supplication for the People of the Frontiers (Ahl- Thughoor)

O God,
bless Muhammad and his Household,
fortify the frontiers of the Muslims
through Your might,
support their defenders
through Your strength,
and lavish upon them gifts
through Your wealth!

O God,
bless Muhammad and his Household,
increase their number,
hone their weapons,
guard their territory,
defend their midst,
unite their throng,
arrange their affair,
send them supplies in a steady string,
undertake Yourself to suffice them with provisions,
support them with victory,
help them with patience,
and give them subtlety in guile!

O God,
bless Muhammad and his Household,
give them the knowledge of that of which they are ignorant,
teach them what they do not know,
and show them what they do not see!

O God,
bless Muhammad and his Household,
make them forget when they meet the enemy
to remember this cheating and delusive world of theirs,
erase from their hearts the thought of enchanting possessions,
place the Garden before their eyes,

and display to their sight that part of it
which You have prepared for them –
the homes of everlastingness
and mansions of honor,
the beautiful houris,
the rivers gushing forth
with all sorts of drinks,
the trees hanging,
low with all kinds of fruits -
lest any of them think of turning his back
or suggest to himself to flee his opponent!

O God,
defeat their enemy through that,
trim their nails from them,
separate them from their weapons,
pull out the firm ties from their hearts,
keep them far away from their stores,
bewilder them in their roads,
turn them astray from their direction,
cut off reinforcements from them,
chop them down in numbers,
fill their hearts with terror,
hold back their hands from stretching forth,
tie back their tongues from speaking,
scatter by them the ones behind them
make them a lesson for those beyond them,
and through their degradation
cut off the hopes of those who come after them!

O God,
make the wombs of their women barren,
dry up the loins of their men,
cut off the breeding of their mounts and their cattle,
and permit not their sky to rain
or their earth to grow!

O God,
through that
strengthen the prowess of the People of Islam,
fortify their cities,
increase their properties,
give them ease
from their fighting
to worship You
and from their warfare
to be alone with You,
so that none will be worshipped
in the regions of the earth but You
and no forehead of theirs may be rubbed in dust
for less than You!

O God,
send out the Muslims of every region on raids against
the idolaters who face them!
Reinforce them with angels in ranks from You,
till the idolaters are routed by them to the end of the land,
slain in Your earth or taken captive,
or till they admit that You are God,
other than whom there is no god,
You alone, who have no associate!

O God,
include in this Your enemies in the regions of the lands,
the Indians, the Byzantines, the Turks,
the Khazars, the Abyssinians, the Nubians,
the Zanjis, the Slavs, the Daylamites,
and the rest of the idol-worshipping nations,
those whose names and attributes are concealed,
but whom You count in Your cognizance
and oversee through Your power!

O God,
distract the idolaters from reaching for the borders of the Muslims

through the idolaters,
bar them from cutting them down
through being cut down,
and hold them back from massing together against them
through dissension!

O God,
empty their hearts of security
and their bodies of strength,
distract their hearts from thinking of stratagems,
make their limbs too feeble for clashing with men,
make them too cowardly for contending with champions,
send against them a troop of Your angels
with some of Your severity
as You did on the Day of Badr,
so that through it You may
cut off their roots,
harvest their thorns,
and disperse their number!

O God,
mix their waters with pestilence
and their foods with maladies,
hurl down their cities,
harass them with peltings,
hinder them through drought,
place their supplies in the most ill-omened part of Your earth
and the farthest from them,
bar them from its fortresses,
and strike them with constant hunger and painful illness!

O God,
if a warrior from the people of Your creed
wars against them
or a struggler from the followers of Your prescriptions
struggles against them
so that Your religion may be the highest,

Your party the strongest,
and Your share the fullest,
cast ease to him,
arrange his affair,
attend to him by granting success,
select for him his companions,
strengthen his back,
lavish upon him livelihood,
give him enjoyment of joyous vitality,
cool for him the heat of yearning,
give him sanctuary from the gloom of loneliness,
make him forget the remembrance of wife and child,
pass along to him an excellent intention,
attend to him with well-being,
make safety his companion,
release him from cowardice,
inspire him with boldness,
provide him with strength,
support him with help,
teach him right conduct and the norms of the Sunna,
point him straight in judgement,
remove from him hypocrisy,
purify him from seeking fame,
and make his thinking and remembrance,
his departing and his staying,
be in You and for You!
When he stands in ranks before Your enemy and his enemy,
make them few in his eye,
diminish their importance in his heart,
give him a turn to prevail over them,
not them a turn to prevail over him!
But if You seal him with felicity
and decree for him martyrdom,
then let it be after
he has exterminated Your enemies by slaying,
captivity has afflicted them,
the borders of the Muslims are secure,
and Your enemy has turned his back in flight!

O God,
and if a Muslim should
take the place of a warrior or a soldier in his home,
attend to those left behind in his absence,
help him with a portion of his property,
assist him with equipment,
hone him for the struggle,
send along with him a supplication for his purpose,
or guard his honor in his absence,
reward him with the like of his reward
measure for measure,
like for like,
and recompense him for his act with an immediate compensation
through which he will hasten to
the profit of what he has sent forth
and the joy of what he has given,
till the present moment takes him to
the bounty You have granted to him
and the generosity You have prepared for him!

O God,
and if the affair of Islam
should worry a Muslim
and the alliance of the idolaters' against Islam
should grieve him,
so that he has the intention to go to war
and is about to enter the struggle,
but frailty keeps him seated,
neediness keeps him waiting,
a mishap delays him,
or an obstruction prevents him from his wish,
write his name
among the worshipers,
make incumbent for him
the reward of the strugglers,
and place him among the ranks
of the martyrs and the righteous!

O God, bless Muhammad, Your slave and Your messenger,
and the Household of Muhammad,
with a blessing high above all other blessings,
towering beyond all other salutations,
a blessing whose end is never reached
and whose number is never cut off,
like the most perfect of Your blessings that has passed
to any one of Your friends!
You are All-kind, Praiseworthy,
the Originator who takes back again,
Accomplisher of what You desire.

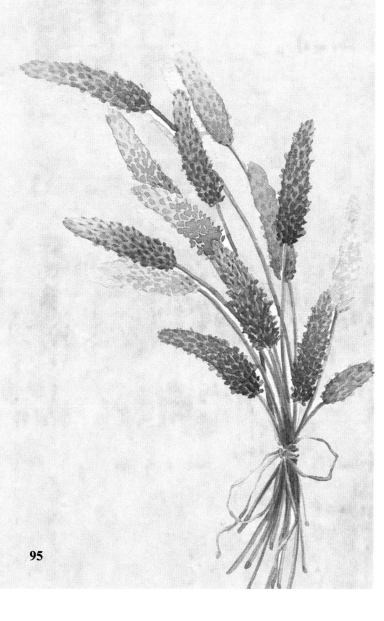

S28 - His Supplication in Fleeing to God

O God,
I showed sincerity by cutting myself off from everything
but You.

I approached You with my whole self.
I averted my face from everyone who needs Your support.
I ceased to ask from any who cannot do without Your bounty.

I saw that the needy who seeks from the needy
is foolish in his opinion,
and misguided in his intellect.

How many people have I seen, my God,
who sought exaltation through other than You
and were abased,
who wanted wealth from someone else
and became poor,
who tried to rise high
and fell down low!

Observing the likes of them
corrects a prudent man;
his taking heed
gives him success;
his choosing the best
guides him to the path of right.

So You, my Master,
are the object of my asking
to the exclusion of all those who are asked
and the patron of my need
to the exclusion of all those from whom requests are made.

You are singled out for my call
before all who are called;
none is associated with You in my hope,
none comes along with You in my supplication,
nor does any join with You within it,
for to You is my appeal.

To You, my God, belongs
the Unity of number,
the property of eternal power,
the excellence of force and strength,
the degree of sublimity and elevation.

Everyone other than You is
the object of compassion in his lifetime,
overcome in his affair,
overwhelmed in his situation,
diverse in states,
constantly changing in attributes.

So You are high exalted
above likenesses and opposites,
proudly magnified
beyond similitudes and rivals!
Glory be to You!
There is no God but You.

S29 - His Supplication when his Provision was Stinted

O God,
You have tried us with
distrust in our provisions
and the expectation of long lives,
until we begged for provisions
from those who are provided
and craved in our expectations
the life-spans of the long-lived!

So bless Muhammad and his Household,
give us a true certainty
that will suffice us the burden of seeking,
and inspire us with a sincere trust
that will release us from the hardship of exertion!

Let Your clear promise in Your Revelation
which You have followed in Your Book with Your oath
cut off our worry
about the provision for which
You have made Yourself responsible
and sever our occupation
with everything
whose sufficiency You have guaranteed!

For You have said –
and Your word is the most truthful truth –
and You have sworn –
and Your oath is the most kept and fulfilled –
In the heaven are your provision
and everything you are promised!
And then You have said,
So by the Lord of heaven and earth,
it is as surely true as that you have speech!

S30 - His Supplication for Help in Repaying Debts

O God,
bless Muhammad and his Household
and release me from a debt
which makes me lose face,
confuses my mind,
disrupts my thinking,
and prolongs my occupation with attending to it!

I seek refuge in You, my Lord,
from worry and thought about debt,
from the distraction and sleeplessness of debt;
so bless Muhammad and his Household
and give me refuge from it!
I seek sanctuary in You, my Lord, from
debt's abasement in life
and its ill effects after death,
so bless Muhammad and his Household
and give me sanctuary from it through
a bountiful plenty
or a continually arriving sufficiency!

O God,
bless Muhammad and his Household
prevent me from extravagance and excess,
put me on the course of generous spending and moderation,
teach me excellent distribution,
hold me back through Your gentleness from squandering,
allow me to attain my provisions through lawful means,
direct my spending toward the gateways of devotion,
and take away from me any possession
which will bring forth pride in me,
lead to insolence,
or drag me in its heels to rebellion!

O God,
make me love the companionship of the poor
and help me be their companion with excellent patience!

Whenever You take away from me
the goods of this perishing world,
store them for me in Your abiding treasuries!

Make this world's broken pieces
which You have conferred upon me
and its goods
which You have quickly granted to me
a way to reach Your neighborhood,
a link to Your nearness,
and a means to Your Garden!
Verily You are Possessor of bounty abounding,
and You are the Munificent, the Generous.

His Supplication in Mentioning and Asking for Repentance

O God,
O He whom the depiction of the describers
fails to describe!

O He beyond whom passes not
the hope of the hopers!

O He with whom is not lost
the wage of the good-doers!

O He who is the ultimate object
of the fear of the worshipers!

O He who is the utmost limit
of the dread of the god-fearing!

This is the station of him
whom sins have passed from hand to hand.
Offenses' reins have led him on,
and Satan has gained mastery over him.
He fell short of what You have commanded
through neglect
and he pursued what You have prohibited
in delusion,

like one ignorant of Your power over him
or one who denies the bounty of Your beneficence toward him,
until, when the eye of guidance was opened for him
and the clouds of blindness were dispelled,

he reckoned that through which he had wronged himself
and reflected upon that in which he had opposed his Lord.
He saw his vast disobedience as vast
and his great opposition as great.

So turned to You,
hoping in You
and ashamed before You,
and he directed his beseeching toward You,
having trust in You.
He repaired to You in his longing
with certitude
and he went straight to You in fear
with sincerity.
His longing was devoid of every object of longing but You,
and his fright departed from every object of fear but You.

So he stood before You pleading,
his eyes turned toward the ground in humbleness,
his head bowed before Your might in lowliness;
he revealed to You in meekness
those secrets of his which You know better than he;
he numbered for You in humility
those sins of his which You count better than he;
he sought help from You
before the dreadful into which he has fallen
in Your knowledge
and the ugly which has disgraced him
in Your judgement:
the sins
whose pleasures have turned their backs
and gone
and whose evil consequences have stayed
and stuck fast.

He will not deny Your justice, my God,
if You punish him,

nor will he consider Your pardon great
if You pardon him and have mercy upon him,
for You are the Generous Lord
for whom the forgiveness of great sins
is nothing great!

O God,
so here I am:
I have come to You
obeying Your command
(for You have commanded supplication)
and asking the fulfillment of Your promise,
(for You have promised to respond)
You have said,
Supplicate Me and I will respond to you.

O God,
so bless Muhammad and his Household,
meet me with Your forgiveness
just as I have met You with my confession,
lift me up from the fatal infirmities of sins
just as I have let myself down before You,
and cover me with Your covering
just as You have shown no haste to take vengeance on me!

O God,
make firm my intention to obey You,
strengthen my insight in worshipping You,
give me the success of works
which will wash away the defilement of offenses,
and take me when You take me
in the creed of Your prophet Muhammad
(upon him be peace).

O God,
I repent to You in this my station from

my sins,
great and small,
my evil deeds,
inward and outward,
my lapses,
past and recent,
with the repentance of one who does not
tell himself that he might disobey
or secretly think that he might return to an offense.

You have said, my God,
in the firm text of Your Book,
that You accept repentance from Your servants,
pardon evil deeds,
and love the repenters,
so accept my repentance
as You have promised,
pardon my evil deeds as
You have guaranteed,
and make obligatory toward me Your love
as You have stipulated!

To You, my Lord, belongs
my stipulation
that I will not return
to what is disliked by You,
my guarantee
that I will not go back
to what You blame,
and my covenant
that I will stay away
from acts of disobedience to You.

O God,
You know better what I have done,
so forgive me what You know
and turn me through Your power to what You love!

O God,
counted against me are
claims that stay in my memory
and claims that I have forgotten,
while all of them remain in
Your eye that does not sleep
and Your knowledge that does not forget!
So compensate their owners,
lighten their load upon me,
lift up their weight from me,
and preserve me from approaching their like!

O God,
but I cannot be faithful to my repentance
without Your preservation,
nor can I refrain from offenses
without Your strength.
So strengthen me with a sufficient strength
and attend to me with a defending preservation!

O God,
if any servant repents to You,
while in Your knowledge of the Unseen he
will break his repentance
and return to his sin and offense,
I seek refuge in You lest I be like that!
So make this my repentance
a repentance
after which I will need no repentance
and a repentance
which will obligate the erasing of what has gone by
and safety in what remains!

O God,
I ask pardon from You for my ignorance,

and I ask You to disregard my evil acts!
So join me to the shelter of Your mercy
through graciousness
and cover me with the covering of Your well-being
through bounteousness!

O God,
I repent to You from everything opposed to Your will
or far from Your love –
the thoughts of my heart,
the glances of my eye,
the tales of my tongue –
with a repentance through which each bodily part will by itself
stay safe from ill consequences with You
and remain secure from Your painful penalties
feared by transgressors!

O God,
so have mercy on
my being alone before You,
the pounding of my heart in dread of You,
the trembling of my limbs in awe of You!
My sins, my God, have stood me in the station
of degradation in Your courtyard.
If I remain silent,
none will speak for me;
if I seek an intercessor,
I am not worthy for intercession.

O God,
bless Muhammad and his Household,
make Your generosity intercede for my offenses,
follow up my evil deeds with Your pardon,
repay me not with the punishment that is my proper repayment,
spread over me Your graciousness,
wrap me in Your covering,
and do with me what is done

by a mighty man,
when a lowly slave pleads to him
and he shows him mercy,
or a rich man,
when a poor slave submits himself
and he raises him to wealth!

O God,
I have no protector against You,
so let Your might be my protector!
I have no intercessor with You,
so let Your bounty be my intercessor!
My offenses have set me quaking,
so let Your pardon give me security!

Not all that I have said rises up from
my ignorance of my evil footsteps
or forgetfulness of my blameworthy acts in the past,
but in order that Your heaven and those within it
and Your earth and those upon it
may hear the remorse which I have professed to You
and the repentance through which I have sought asylum with You.

Then perhaps one of them, through Your mercy,
may show mercy upon my evil situation
or be seized by tenderness for my evil state.
There may come from him for my sake
a supplication to which You give ear
more than to my supplication
or an intercession surer with You
than my intercession
through which I may be delivered from Your wrath
and attain to Your good pleasure!

O God,
if remorse is a repentance toward You,

then I am the most remorseful of the remorseful!
If refraining from disobedience is a turning back to You,
then I am the first of those who turn back!
If praying for forgiveness alleviates sins,
surely I am one of those who pray for Your forgiveness!

O God,
as You have commanded repentance
and guaranteed acceptance,
as You have urged supplication,
and promised to respond,
so also bless Muhammad and his Household,
accept my repentance,
and return me not to the returning place
of disappointment in Your mercy!
Surely You are Ever-turning toward the sinners,
All-compassionate toward the offenders who turn back!

O God,
bless Muhammad and his Household
just as You have guided us by him!
Bless Muhammad and his Household
just as You have rescued us through him!
Bless Muhammad and his Household,
with a blessing that will intercede for us
on the Day of Resurrection,
the day of neediness toward You!
You are powerful over everything,
and that is easy for You!

S32 - His Supplication in the Night Prayer

His Supplication for himself in Confessing Sins after Finishing the Night Prayer

O God,
O Possessor of
kingdom perpetual in everlastingness,
authority invincible without armies or helpers,

might abiding through eons past,
years gone by,
times and days elapsed!

Your authority is mighty
with a might that knows no bound by being first
nor utmost end by being last!

Your kingdom towers high with a towering
before which all things fall down without reaching its term;

the least of it which You have kept to Yourself is not reached
by the furthest description of the describers!

Attributes go astray in You,
descriptions fall apart below You,
the subtlest of imaginations are bewildered
by Your magnificence!

So are You:
God, the First in Your firstness,
and so are You everlastingly.
You do not pass away.

But I am the slave,
feeble in works,
immense in hopes.
The tying links are outside my hand,
except what is tied by Your mercy;
the bonds of hopes have been cut away from me,
except the pardon to which I hold fast.

Little on my part is
the obedience towards You upon which I
count, and great against me
the disobedience towards You to which I have
reverted. But pardoning Your slave will not
constrainYou, even if he be bad,
so pardon me!

O God,
Your knowledge watches over hidden works,
every covered thing is exposed before Your awareness,
the intricacies of things are not concealed from You,
and unseen mysteries slip not away from You.

But over me Your enemy has gained mastery:
He asked a delay from You to lead me astray,
and You gave him the delay!
He asked a respite from You until the Day of Doom to misguide me,
and You gave him the respite!

So he threw me down,
though I had fled to You from
small, ruinous sins
and great, deadly works,
until, when I had yielded to disobeying You
and merited Your anger through my bad efforts,
he turned the bridle of his treachery away from me,

met me with the word of his ingratitude,
undertook to be quit of me,
turned his back to flee from me,
threw me to the desert of Your wrath alone,
and sent me as an outcast
into the courtyard of Your vengeance.

There is no intercessor to intercede for me with You,
no protector to make me feel secure against You,
no fortress to veil me from You,
no shelter in which to seek asylum apart from You!

This is the station of him who takes refuge with You,
the place of the confessor to You:
Let not Your bounty be too narrow for me,
let not Your pardon fall short of me!
Let me not be the most disappointed
of Your repentant servants,
nor the most despairing
of those who come to You with expectations!
Forgive me,
surely You are the best of the forgivers!

O God,
You commanded me,
and I refrained,
You prohibited me,
and I committed.
evil thoughts tempted me to offend,
and I was negligent.

I cannot call upon daytime to witness my fasting,
nor can I seek sanctuary in night because of my vigil;
no Sunna praises me for keeping it alive,
only Your obligations,
he who neglects which has perished.

I cannot seek access to You
through the excellence of a supererogatory work,
given the many duties of Your obligations
of which I have been heedless
and the stations of Your bounds which I have transgressed,
thereby violating sacred things and committing great sins,
though You have given me safety from their disgraces as a covering.

This is the station of him who is
ashamed of himself before You,
angry with himself,
and satisfied with You.
He meets You
with a humble soul,
a neck bent down,
a back heavy with offenses,
hesitating between longing for You and fear of You.

You are the most worthy of those in whom he might hope,
the most deserving for him to dread and fear.
So give me, my Lord, what I hope for,
make me secure against what frightens me,
and act kindly toward me with the kindly act of mercy!
Surely You are the most generous
of those from whom are asked!

O God,
since You have covered me with Your pardon
and shielded me with Your bounty
in the abode of annihilation and the presence of equals,
grant me sanctuary from the disgraces of the Abode of Subsistence
at the standing places of the Witnesses
(the angels brought nigh,
the messengers honored,
the martyrs, the righteous)

before the neighbor
from whom I have hidden my evil deeds
and the womb relative
before whom I feel ashamed in my secret thoughts!

I trust them not, my Lord,
to cover me over,
but I trust You, my Lord,
to forgive me!
You are the most worthy of those in whom confidence is had,
the most giving of those who are besought,
and the most clement of those from whom mercy is asked.
So have mercy upon me!

O God,
You caused me to descend as mean water
from loins of narrow bones and tight passages
into a constricted womb
which You had covered with veils;
You turned me about from state to state
until You took me to the completion of the form
and fixed within me the bodily parts,
as You have described in Your Book:
a drop,
then a clot,
then a tissue,
then bones,
then You garmented the bones with flesh,
then You produced me as another creature
as You willed.

Then, when I needed Your provision,
and could not do without the aid of Your bounty,
You appointed for me a nourishment
from the bounty of the food and drink
which You bestowed upon Your handmaid
in whose belly You gave me to rest

113

and in the lodging of whose womb
You deposited me.

Had You entrusted me in those states, my Lord,
to my own force
or driven me to have recourse to my own strength,
force would have been removed from me
and strength taken far away.

So You have fed me through Your bounty
with the food of the Good, the Gentle;
You have done that for me in graciousness toward me
up to this my present point.
I do not lack Your goodness,
nor does Your benefaction keep me waiting.
Yet with all that,
my trust has not become firm enough
that I might free myself
for that which is more favored by You.

Satan has taken possession of my reins
through my distrust and frail certainty.
I complain of his evil neighborhood with me
and my soul's obedience toward him!
I ask You to preserve me against his domination,
and I plead with You to turn his trickery away from me!

I ask You
to make the path to my provision easy,
since to You belongs praise for
Your beginning with immense favors
and Your inspiring gratitude
for beneficence and bestowing favor!
Bless Muhammad and his Household,
and make the way to my provision easy for me!
[I ask You] to make me content

with Your ordainment for me,
to make me satisfied with my lot
in that which You have apportioned for me
and to place what has gone of my body and my life-span
into the path of Your obedience!
Surely You are the Best of providers!

O God, I seek refuge in You
from the Fire
through which You are harsh
toward him who disobeys You
and by which You have threatened
him who turns away from Your good pleasure;
from the Fire
whose light is darkness,
whose ease is pain,
and whose far is near;
from the Fire
parts of which devour parts
and parts of which leap upon parts;

from the Fire which
leaves bones decayed
and lets its people drink boiling water;
from the Fire which
'does not spare him who pleads to it,'
has no mercy on him who seeks sympathy from it,
and has no power to relieve him
who humbles himself before it
and yields himself to it;
it meets its inhabitants with the hottest that it possesses:
painful punishment and intense noxiousness.

I seek refuge in You from
its gaping-jawed scorpions,
its scraping-toothed serpents,
and its drinks, which

tear apart the intestines and hearts of its inhabitants
and root out their marrows.
I ask guidance from You
to that which will keep far from it
and make it retreat!

O God,
bless Muhammad and his Household,
grant me sanctuary from it through the bounty of Your mercy,
release me from my stumbles through Your good releasing,
and abandon me not,
O Best of the sanctuary-granters!

O God,
You protect from the disliked,
give the good,
do what You will,
and You are powerful over everything.

O God,
bless Muhammad and his Household
when the pious are mentioned
and bless Muhammad and his Household
as long as night and day come and go
with a blessing
whose replenishment is never cut off
and whose number cannot be counted,
a blessing
that will fill up the air
and crowd the earth and the heaven!

God bless him
until he is well pleased
and God bless him and his Household
after good pleasure
with a blessing that has neither bound

nor utmost limit!
O Most Merciful of the merciful!

S33 - His Supplication in Asking for the Best

O God,
I ask from You the best in Your knowledge,
so bless Muhammad and his Household
and decree for me the best!

Inspire us with knowledge to choose the best
and make that a means to
being pleased with what You have decreed for us
and submitting to what You have decided!
Banish from us the doubt of misgiving
and confirm us with the certainty of the sincere!

Visit us not with incapacity
to know what You have chosen, lest we
despise Your measuring out,
dislike the place of Your good pleasure,
and incline toward that which is
further from good outcome
and nearer to the opposite of well-being!

Make us love what we dislike
in Your decree
and make easy for us what we find difficult
in Your decision!

Inspire us to yield
to that which You bring upon us by Your will,
lest we
love the delay of what You have hastened
and the hastening of what You have delayed,
dislike what You love,
and choose what You dislike!

Seal us with that which is most praised in outcome
and most generous in issue!
Surely You give generous gain,
bestow the immense,
do what You will,
and You are powerful over everything.

S34 - His Supplication when Afflicted

His Supplication when he was Afflicted or saw Someone Afflicted with the Disgrace of Sin

O God,
to You belongs praise for
Your covering over after Your knowledge
and Your pardon after Your awareness!
Each of us has committed faults,
but You have not made him notorious,
done indecencies,
but You have not disgraced him,
and covered over evil deeds,
but You have not pointed to him.

How many are Your prohibited acts
which we have performed,
Your commandments of which You have told us
which we have transgressed,
the evil deeds
which we have earned,
the offenses
which we have committed!
You see them
to the exclusion of all observers;
You have the power to make them public
above all the powerful!
By giving us safety
You have veiled their eyes
and stopped their ears.

So make
the shameful things You have covered over
and the inward reality You have concealed
our admonisher,
a restrainer upon bad character traits and committing offenses,
and a striving toward the repentance that erases [sins]

and the praiseworthy path!

Bring the time of striving near
and visit us not with heedlessness of You!
Surely we are Your beseechers,
the repenters of sins.

And bless Your chosen, O God, from Your creation,
Muhammad and his descendants,
the friends selected from among Your creatures, the pure,
and make us listeners to them and obeyers,
as You have commanded!

S35 - His Supplication in Satisfaction with the Decree

His Supplication in Satisfaction when he Looked upon the Companions of this World

Praise belongs to God
in satisfaction with God's decision!
I bear witness that
God has apportioned the livelihoods of His servants with justice and undertaken bounty for all
His creatures.

O God,
bless Muhammad and his Household,
tempt me not with what You have given to Your creatures
and tempt them not with what You have withheld from me.
Lest I envy Your creatures
and despise Your decision!

O God,
bless Muhammad and his Household,
delight my soul through Your decree,
expand my breast through the instances of Your decision,
give to me a trust through which I may admit
that Your decree runs only to the best,
and let my gratitude to You
for what You have taken away from me
be more abundant than my gratitude to You
for what You have conferred upon me!

Preserve me from imagining any meanness
in someone who is destitute
or imagining any superiority
in someone who possesses wealth,
for the noble is he
whom obedience to You has ennobled
and the exalted is he
whom worship of You has exalted!

So bless Muhammad and his Household,
give us to enjoy a wealth
which does not run out,
confirm us with an exaltation
which will never be lost,
and let us roam freely
in the kingdom of everlastingness!
Surely You are the One, the Unique, the Eternal Refuge;
You have not begotten,
nor have You been begotten,
and equal to You is not any one

S36 - His Supplication upon Hearing Thunder

His Supplication when he Looked upon Clouds and Lightening and Heard the Sound of Thunder

O God,
these are two of Your signs
and these are two of Your helpers.
They rush to obey You
with beneficial mercy
or injurious vengeance,
so rain not down upon us from them
the evil rain
and clothe us not through them
in the garment of affliction!

O God,
bless Muhammad and his Household,
send down upon us the benefit of these clouds
and their blessing,
turn away from us their harm and their injury,
strike us not through them with blight,
and loose not upon our livelihoods any bane!

O God,
if You have incited them as vengeance
and loosed them in anger,
we seek sanctuary with You from Your wrath
and implore You in asking Your pardon!
So incline with wrath
toward the idolaters
and set the millstone of Your vengeance
turning upon the heretics!

O God,
take away the barrenness of our lands

with Your watering,
dislodge the malice from our breasts
with Your providing,
distract us not from You
through other than You,
and cut none of us off
from the stuff of Your goodness,
for the rich is he to whom You have given riches,
and the safe he whom You have protected!

No one has any defense against You,
nor any means to bar Your penalty.
You decide what You will
for whom You will
and You decree what You desire
for any whom You desire!

So to You belongs praise
for protecting us from affliction
and to You belongs thanks
for conferring upon us blessings,
a praise which will leave behind the praise of the praisers,
a praise which will fill the earth and the heaven!

Surely You are the All-kind through immense kindnesses,
the Giver of abounding favors,
the Accepter of small praise,
the Grateful for little gratitude,
the Beneficent, the Benevolent,
Possessor of graciousness!
There is no god but You;
unto You is the homecoming.

S37 - His Supplication in Giving Thanks

His Supplication when Confessing his Shortcomings in Giving Thanks

O God,
no one reaches a limit in thanking You
without acquiring that of Your beneficence
which enjoins upon him thanksgiving,

nor does anyone reach a degree in obeying You,
even if he strives,
without falling short of what You deserve
because of Your bounty.

The most thankful of Your servants
has not the capacity to thank You,
and the most worshipful of them
falls short of obeying You.

To none of them is due
Your forgiveness through what he himself deserves
or Your good pleasure for his own merit.

When You forgive someone,
it is through Your graciousness,
and when You are pleased with someone,
it is through Your bounty.

You show gratitude
for the paltry for which You show gratitude
and You reward
the small act in which You are obeyed,
so that it seems as if Your servants' thanksgiving
for which You have made incumbent their reward

and made great their repayment
is an affair
from which they could have held back without You,
and hence You will recompense them,
and whose cause is not in Your hand,
and hence You will repay them.

Nay, my God, You had power over their affair
before they had power to worship You,
and You had prepared their reward
before they began to obey You;
and that because Your wont is bestowal of bounty,
Your custom beneficence,
Your way pardon.

So all creatures confess
that You wrong not him whom You punish
and bear witness
that You bestow bounty upon him whom You pardon.
Each admits
that he has fallen short of what You merit.

Had Satan not misled them from Your obedience,
no disobeyer would have disobeyed You,
and had he not shown falsehood to them in the likeness of truth
no strayer would have gone astray from Your path.

So glory be to You!
How manifest is Your generosity
in dealing with him who obeys or disobeys You!
You show gratitude to the obedient
for that which You undertake for him,
and You grant a respite to the disobedient
in that within which You are able to hurry him.

You give to each of them
that which is not his due,
and You bestow bounty upon each
in that wherein his works fall short.

Were You to counterbalance for the obedient servant
that which You Yourself had undertaken,
he would be on the point of losing Your reward
and seeing the end of Your favor,
but through Your generosity You have repaid him
for a short, perishing term
with a long, everlasting term,
and for a near, vanishing limit
with an extended, abiding limit.

Then You do not visit him with a settling of accounts
for Your provision
through which he gained strength to obey You,
nor do You force him to make reckonings
for the organs he employed
to find the means to Your forgiveness.
Were You to do that to him,
it would take away
everything for which he had labored
and all wherein he had exerted himself
as repayment for the smallest of Your benefits
and kindnesses,
and he would remain hostage before You
for Your other favors.
So how can he deserve something of Your reward?
Indeed, how?

This, my God, is the state of him who obeys You
and the path of him who worships You.
But as for him who disobeys Your command
and goes against Your prohibition,
You do not hurry him to Your vengeance,

so that he may seek to replace
his state in disobeying You
with the state of turning back to obey You,
though he deserved from the time he set out to disobey You
every punishment which You have prepared
for all Your creatures.

Through each chastisement
which You have kept back from him
and each penalty of Your vengeance and Your punishment
which You have delayed from him,
You have refrained from Your right
and shown good pleasure
in place of what You have made obligatory.

So who is more generous, my God, than You?
And who is more wretched than he who perishes
in spite of You?
Indeed, who?
You are too blessed to be described
by any but beneficence
and too generous for any but justice
to be feared from You!
There is no dread that You will be unjust
toward him who disobeys You,
nor any fear of Your neglecting to reward him who
satisfies You.
So bless Muhammad and his Household,
give me my hope,
and increase me in that of Your guidance
through which I may be successful in my works!
Surely You are All-kind, Generous.

S38 - His Supplication in Asking Pardon

His Supplication in Asking Pardon for Misdeeds to God's Servants and for Falling Short in their Rights and that his Neck be Set Free from the Fire

O God,
I ask pardon from You for
the person wronged in my presence
whom I did not help,
the favor conferred upon me
for which I returned no thanks,
the evildoer who asked pardon from me
and whom I did not pardon,
the needy person who asked from me
and whom I preferred not over myself,
the right of a believer who possesses a right incumbent upon me
which I did not fulfil,
the fault of a believer which became evident to me
and which I did not conceal,
and every sin which presented itself to me
and which I failed to avoid.

I ask pardon, my God,
for all of these and their likes,
with an asking of pardon in remorse
which may act as an admonisher
against similar things ahead of me.

So bless Muhammad and his Household
and make my remorse for the slips
into which I have fallen
and my determination to refrain from the evil deeds
which present themselves to me
a repentance which will make Your love for me obligatory
O lover of those who repent!

S39 - His Supplication in Seeking Pardon and Mercy

O God,
bless Muhammad and his Household,
break my passion for every unlawful thing,
take away my craving for any sin,
and bar me from harming any believer, male or female,
and any Muslim, male or female!

O God,
if any of Your servants should harm me in what You have forbidden
or violate me in what You have interdicted,
and if he should pass into death with my complaint
or I come to have a complaint against him while he is alive,
forgive him what he did to me
and pardon him that through which he turned his back on me!
Inquire not from him about what he committed toward me
and expose him not through what he earned by me!
Make my open-handedness in pardoning such servants
and my contribution in charity toward them
the purest charity of the charitable
and the highest gift of those seeking nearness to You!

Recompense me for my pardoning them with Your pardon
and for my supplicating for them with Your mercy
so that each one of us may gain felicity through Your bounty
and each may attain deliverance through Your kindness!

O God,
if there is a servant from among Your servants whom
an ill visits on my account,
a harm touches from my direction,
or a wrong overtakes through me or because of me,
and should I fail to take care of his right
or go before him [in death] with his complaint,
bless Muhammad and his Household,

satisfy him toward me through Your wealth,
and give him his full right from Yourself!

Then protect me from what Your decision mandates
and save me from what Your justice decides,
for my strength cannot bear Your vengeance
and my obedience cannot stand up to Your displeasure!
If You recompense me with the right,
You will destroy me,
and if You do not shield me in Your mercy,
You will lay me waste.

O God,
I ask You to grant, my God,
that whose giving will not decrease You,
and I ask You to carry
that whose carrying will not weigh You down:

My God, I ask You to give my soul,
which You did not create
to keep Yourself from evil
nor to find the way to profit.
No, You brought it forth
to demonstrate Your power over its like
and to provide an argument against its similar.

I ask You to carry those of my sins
whose carrying weighs me down
and I seek help from You in
that whose heaviness oppresses me.

So bless Muhammad and his Household,
give to me my soul in spite of its wrongdoing,
and appoint Your mercy to carry my burden!
How many evildoers Your mercy has overtaken!

How many wrongdoers Your pardon has embraced!

So bless Muhammad and his Household
and make me the model of him whom You have
aroused through Your forbearance
from the deadly infirmities of the Senders
and saved through Your giving success
from the tangled plights of the sinners,
so that I may rise up
freed by Your pardon from the bonds of Your displeasure
and released by Your benefaction from the ties of Your justice!

Surely if You do that, my God,
You will do it to one who does not
deny deserving Your punishment
or acquit himself from merit for Your vengeance.

Do that, my God, for one
whose fear of You is greater
than his craving from You,
whose hopelessness of deliverance
is firmer than his hope for salvation!
Not that his hopelessness is despair,
nor that his expectation is deluded.
No, rather his good deeds are few
among his evil deeds
and his arguments are frail
in face of everything due from his acts.

But You, my God, are worthy that
the righteous not be deluded concerning You
and the sinners not lose hope in You,
for You are the All-mighty Lord who
holds back His bounty from none
and takes His full right from no one.

High exalted is Your mention
above those mentioned!
Holy are Your names
beyond those described!
Spread is Your favor
among all creatures!
Yours is the praise for that,
O Lord of the worlds!

S40 - His Supplication when Death was Mentioned

His Supplication when Someone's Death was Announced to him or when he Remembered Death

O God,
Bless Muhammad and his Household,
spare us drawn out expectations
and cut them short in us through sincerity of works,
that we may not hope expectantly for
completing an hour after an hour,
closing a day after a day,
joining a breath to a breath,
or overtaking a step with a step!

Keep us safe from the delusions of expectations,
make us secure from their evils,
set up death before us in display.
and let not our remembering of it come and go!

Appoint for us from among the righteous works a work
through which we will feel the homecoming to You as slow
and crave a quick joining with You,
so that death may be
our intimate abode with which we are intimate,
our familiar place toward which we yearn,
and our next of kin whose coming we love!

When You bring it to us
and send it down upon us,
make us happy with it as a visitor,
comfort us with its arrival,
make us not wretched through entertaining it,
degrade us not through its visit,
and appoint it one of the gates to Your forgiveness
and the keys to Your mercy!

135

Make us die
guided, not astray,
obedient, not averse,
repentant, not disobedient or persisting,
O He who guarantees the repayment of the good-doers
and seeks to set right the work of the corrupt!

S41 - His Supplication in Asking for Covering and Protection

O God,
bless Muhammad and his Household,
spread for me the bed of Your honor,
bring me to the watering holes of Your mercy,
set me down in the midst of Your Garden,
stamp me not with rejection by You,
deprive me not through disappointment by You,

settle not accounts with me for what I have committed,
make no reckoning with me for what I have earned,
display not what I have hidden,
expose not what I have covered over,
weigh not my works on the scales of fairness,
and make not my tidings known to the eyes of the crowd!

Conceal from them
everything whose unfolding would shame me
and roll up before them
all which would join me to disgrace with You!

Ennoble my degree through Your good pleasure,
perfect my honor through Your forgiveness,
rank me among the companions of the right hand,
direct me to the roads of the secure,
place me in the throng of the triumphant,
and through me let the sessions of the righteous thrive!
Amen, Lord of the worlds!

S42 - His Supplication Upon Completing a Reading of the Qur'an

O God,
You have helped me complete Your Book,
which You sent down as a light
and appointed as a guardian
over every book You have sent down,
preferring it over every narrative
which You have recounted,

a separator, through which You have separated Your
lawful from Your unlawful,
a Qur'an, through which You have made plain the
approaches to Your ordinances,
a book, which You have distinguished very distinctly
for Your servants,
a revelation, which You have sent down,
a sending down,
upon Your prophet Muhammad
(Your blessings be upon him and his Household).

You appointed it
a light through following which we may be guided
from the shadows of error and ignorance, a healing
for him
who turns ear toward hearing it
with the understanding of attestation,
a just balance
whose tongue does not incline away from truth,
a light of guidance
whose proof is not extinguished before the
witnesses,
and a guidepost of deliverance, so that
he who repairs straightway to its prescription
will not go astray
and he who clings to its preservation's handhold

will not be touched by the hands of disasters.

O God,
since You have given us help to recite it
and made smooth the roughness of our tongues
through the beauty of its expression,
place us among those who
observe it as it should be observed,
serve You by adhering in submission
to the firm text of its verses,
and seek refuge in admitting both its ambiguous parts
and the elucidations of its clear signs!

O God,
You sent it down upon Your prophet Muhammad
(God bless him and his household) in summary form,
You inspired him with the science of its wonders
to complement it,
You made us the heirs of its knowledge as
interpreters,
You made us to surpass
him who is ignorant of its knowledge,
and You gave us strength over it
to raise us above those not able to carry it.

O God,
just as You have appointed our hearts
as its carriers
and made known to us through Your mercy
its nobility and excellence,
so also bless Muhammad, its preacher,
and his Household, its guardians,
and place us among those who confess that it has come from You,
lest doubt about attesting to it assail us,
or deviation from its straightforward path shake us!

O God,
bless Muhammad and his Household
and make us one of those who
hold fast to its cord,
seek haven from its ambiguities in its
fortified stronghold,
rest in the shadow of its wing,
find guidance in the brightness of its morning,
follow the shining of its disclosure,
acquire light from its lamp,
and beg not guidance from any other!

O God,
just as through it
You have set up Muhammad
as a guidepost to point to You
and through his Household
You have made clear
Your good pleasure's roads to You,
so also bless Muhammad and his Household
and make the Qur'an
our mediation to the noblest stations
of Your honor,
a ladder by which we may climb
to the place of safety,
a cause for our being repaid
with deliverance at the Plain of Resurrection,
and a means whereby we may reach
the bliss of the House of Permanence!

O God,
bless Muhammad and his Household,
lessen for us through the Qur'an the weight of heavy sins,
give to us the excellent qualities of the pious,
and make us follow the tracks of those who stood before
You in the watches of the night and the ends of the day,

such that You purify us from every defilement
through its purification
and make us to follow the tracks of
those who have taken illumination from its light
and whom expectation has not distracted from works,
cutting them off through its delusions' deceptions!

O God,
bless Muhammad and his Household
and appoint the Qur'an
for us an intimate
in the shadows of nights
and a guardian
against the instigations of Satan
and confusing thoughts,
for our feet an obstruction
from passing to acts of disobedience,
for our tongues a silencer without blight
preventing a plunge into falsehood,
for our limbs a restrainer
from committing sins,
and for the scrutiny of heedfulness
rolled up in heedlessness
an unroller,
such that You attach to our hearts
the understanding of the Qur'an's wonders
and its restraining similitudes
which immovable mountains in all their solidity
were too weak to carry!

O God,
bless Muhammad and his Household
and through the Qur'an
make permanent the rightness
of our outward selves,
veil the ideas of confusing thoughts
from the soundness of our innermost minds,
wash away the dirt of our hearts

and the ties of our heavy sins,
gather our scattered affairs,
quench the thirst of our burning heat
in the standing place of the presentation to You,
and clothe us in the robes of security
on the Day of the Greatest Terror at our uprising!

O God,
bless Muhammad and his Household
and through the Qur'an
redress our lack - our destitution in poverty -
drive toward us the comforts of life
and an abundance of plentiful provisions,
turn aside blameworthy character traits
and base moral qualities,
and preserve us from the pit of unbelief
and the motives for hypocrisy,
such that the Qur'an may be for us
at the resurrection a leader
to Your good pleasure
and Your gardens,
for us in this world a protector
against Your displeasure
and transgressing Your bounds
and for what is with You a witness
by its declaring lawful the lawful
and its declaring unlawful the unlawful!

O God,
bless Muhammad and his Household
and through the Qur'an make easy for our souls at death
the distress of the driving,
the effort of the moaning,
and the succession of the rattling,
when souls reach the throats
and it is said, 'Where is the enchanter?';
when the angel of death discloses himself
to seize them from behind the veils of unseen things,

letting loose at them from the bow of destinies
the arrows of the terror of lonesome separation,
and mixing for them from sudden death
a cup poisoned to the taste;
and when departure and release for the hereafter come close to us,
works become collars around the necks,
and the graves become the haven
until the appointed time of the Day of Encounter!

O God,
bless Muhammad and his Household,
make blessed for us the arrival at the house of decay and the drawn
out residence between the layers of the earth,
appoint the graves, after separation from this world,
the best of our way stations,
make roomy for us through Your mercy the narrowness of our tombs,
and disgrace us not among those present at the Resurrection
through our ruinous sins!

Through the Qur'an
have mercy upon the lowliness of our station
at the standing place of presentation to You,
make firm the slips of our feet
during the shaking of the bridge across hell
on the day of passage over it,
illuminate the darkness of our graves
before the Uprising,
and deliver us from every distress on the Day of Resurrection
and from the hardships of terrors on the Day of Disaster!

Whiten our faces
on the day when the faces of wrongdoers are blackened
during the Day of Regret and Remorse,
appoint love for us in the breasts of the faithful,
and make not life for us troublesome!

O God,
bless Muhammad, Your servant and Your messenger,
just as He delivered Your message,
executed Your command,
and counselled Your servants!

O God,
on the Day of Resurrection make our Prophet
(Your blessings be upon him and his Household)
the nearest of the prophets to You in seat,
the ablest of them before You with intercession,
the greatest of them with You in measure,
and the most eminent of them with You in rank!

O God,
bless Muhammad and the Household of Muhammad,
ennoble his edifice,
magnify his proof,
make weighty his balance, accept his intercession,
bring near his mediation, whiten his face,
complete his light,
and raise his degree!

Make us live according to his Sunna,
make us die in his creed,
take us on his road,
make us travel his path,
place us among the people who obey him,
muster us in his band,
lead us to up his pool,
and give us to drink of his cup!

And bless Muhammad and his Household,
with a blessing

through which You will take him to the most excellent
of Your good, Your bounty, and Your generosity
for which he hopes!
You are Possessor of boundless mercy
and generous bounty.

O God,
repay him for
Your messages which he delivered,
Your signs which he passed on,
the good counsel he gave to Your servants,
and the struggle he undertook in Your way,
with the best You have repaid any of Your angels brought nigh
and Your prophets sent out and chosen!
And upon him and his Household,
the good, the pure,
be peace, God's mercy, and His blessings!

S43 - His Supplication when he Looked at the New Crescent Moon

O obedient creature,
speedy and untiring,
frequenter of the mansions of determination,
moving about in the sphere of governance!

I have faith in Him who
lights up darknesses through You,
illuminates jet-black shadows by You,
appointed You one of the signs of His kingdom
and one of the marks of His authority,
and humbled You through increase and decrease,
rising and setting,
illumination and eclipse.
In all of this You are obedient to Him,
prompt toward His will.

Glory be to Him!
How wonderful is what He has arranged in Your situation!
How subtle what He has made for Your task!
He has made You the key
to a new month
for a new situation.

So I ask God, my Lord and Your Lord,
my Creator and Your Creator,
my Determiner and Your Determiner,
my Form-giver and Your Form-giver,
that He bless Muhammad and his Household
and appoint You
a crescent of blessings not effaced by days
and of purity not defiled by sins;

a crescent of security from blights

and of safety from evil deeds;
a crescent of auspiciousness containing no misfortune,
of prosperity accompanied by no adversity,
of ease not mixed with difficulty,
of good unstained by evil;
a crescent of security and faith,
favor and good-doing,
safety and submission!

O God,
bless Muhammad and his Household,
place us among
the most satisfied of those
over whom the crescent has risen,
the purest of those
who have looked upon it,
the most fortunate of those
who have worshipped You under it;
give us the success during [the new month] to repent,
preserve us within it from misdeeds,
guard us therein from pursuing disobedience to You,

allot to us within it thanksgiving for Your favor,
clothe us during it in the shields of well-being,
and complete for us Your kindness
by perfecting therein obedience to You!
Surely You are All-kind, Praiseworthy.
And bless Muhammad and his Household, the good, the pure.

S44 - His Supplication for the Coming of the Month of Ramadan

Praise belongs to God who guided us to His praise
and placed us among the people of praise,
that we might be among the thankful for His beneficence
and that He might recompense us for that
with the recompense of the good-doers!

And praise belongs to God who
showed favor to us through His religion,
singled us out for His creed,
and directed us onto the roads of His beneficence,
in order that through His kindness we might travel upon them
to His good pleasure,
a praise which He will accept from us
and through which He will be pleased with us!

And praise belongs to God
who appointed among those roads His month,
the month of Ramadan,
the month of fasting,
the month of submission,
the month of purity,
the month of putting to test,
the month of standing in prayer,
in which the Qur'an was sent down
as guidance to the people,
and as clear signs
of the Guidance and the Separator!

He clarified its excellence over other months
by the many sacred things
and well-known excellencies
which He placed therein,
for He made unlawful in it
what He declared lawful in others

to magnify it,
He prohibited foods and drinks in it
to honor it,
and He appointed for it a clear time which He
(majestic and mighty is He)
allows not to be set forward
and accepts not to be placed behind.

Then He made one of its nights
surpass the nights
of a thousand months
and named it the Night of Decree;
in it the angels and the Spirit descend
by the leave of their Lord upon every command,
a peace constant in blessings
until the rising of the dawn
upon whomsoever He will of His servants
according to the decision He has made firm.

O God,
bless Muhammad and his Household,
inspire us
with knowledge of its excellence,
veneration of its inviolability,
and caution against what You have forbidden within it,
and help us to fast in it
by our restraining our limbs
from acts of disobedience toward You
and our employing them
in that which pleases You,
so that we lend not our ears to idle talk
and hurry not with our eyes to diversion,

we stretch not our hands toward the forbidden
and stride not with our feet toward the prohibited,
our bellies hold only what You have made lawful
and our tongues speak only

149

what You have exemplified,
we undertake nothing but
what brings close to Your reward
and pursue nothing but
what protects from Your punishment!
Then rid all of that from
the false show of the false showers
and the fame seeking of the fame seekers,
lest we associate therein anything with You
or seek therein any object of desire but You!

O God,
bless Muhammad and his Household,
in it make us attend
to the appointed moments of the five prayers within
the bounds You have set,
the obligations You have decreed,
the duties You have assigned,
and the times You have specified;

and in the prayers
make us alight in the station of
the keepers of their stations,
the guardians of their pillars,
their performers in their times,
as Your servant and Your messenger set down in his Sunna
(Your blessings be upon him and his Household)
in their bowings,
their prostrations,
and all their excellent acts,
with the most complete and ample ritual purity
and the most evident and intense humility!

Give us success in this month to
tighten our bonds of kin with devotion and gifts,
attend to our neighbors with bestowal and giving,
rid our possessions from claims,

purify them through paying the alms,
go back to him who has gone far from us,
treat justly him who has wronged us,
make peace with him who shows enmity toward us
(except him who is regarded as
an enemy in You and for You,
for he is the enemy whom we will not befriend,
the party whom we will not hold dear),

and seek nearness to You through blameless works
which will purify us from sins
and preserve us from renewing faults,
so that none of Your angels will bring for You
the kinds of obedience
and sorts of nearness-seeking
unless they be less than what we bring!

O God,
I ask You by the right of this month
and by the right of him who worships You within it
from its beginning to the time of its passing,
whether angel You have brought nigh to You,
prophet You have sent,
or righteous servant You have singled out,
that You bless Muhammad and his Household,
make us worthy of the generosity
You have promised Your friends,
make incumbent for us
what You have made incumbent
for those who go to great lengths in obeying You,
and place us in the ranks of those
who deserve through Your mercy the highest elevation!

O God,
bless Muhammad and his Household,
turn us aside from
deviation in professing Your Unity,

falling short in magnifying You,
in Your religion,
blindness toward Your path,
heedlessness of Your inviolability,
and being deceived by Your enemy, the accursed Satan!

O God,
bless Muhammad and his Household,
and when in every night of this month's nights
You have necks
which Your pardon will release
and Your forgiveness disregard,
place our necks among those necks
and place us among
the best folk and companions
of this our month!

O God,
bless Muhammad and his Household,
efface our sins
along with the effacing of its crescent moon,
and make us pass forth from the ill effects of our acts
with the passing of its days,
until it leaves us behind,
while within it You have purified us of offenses
and rid us of evil deeds!

O God,
bless Muhammad and his Household,
and should we go off to one side in this month,
set us aright;
should we swerve,
point us straight;
and should Your enemy Satan enwrap us,
rescue us from him!

O God,
fill this month with our worship of You,
adorn its times with our obedience toward You,
help us during its daytime with its fast,
and in its night with prayer and pleading toward You,
humility toward You,
and lowliness before You,
so that its daytime may not bear witness
against our heedlessness,
nor its night against our neglect!

O God,
make us like this in the other months and days
as long as You give us life,
and place us among Your righteous servants,
those who shall inherit Paradise,
therein dwelling forever,
those who give what they give,
while their hearts quake,
that they are returning to their Lord,
those who vie in good works,
outracing to them!

O God,
bless Muhammad and his Household
in every time, in all moments, and in every state,
to the number that You have blessed whomsoever
You have blessed
and to multiples of all that, through multiples
which none can count but You!
Surely You are Accomplisher of what You desire.

S45 – His Supplication in Bidding Farewell to the Month of Ramadan

O God,
O He who desires no repayment!
O He who shows no remorse at bestowal!
O He who rewards not His servant tit for tat!

Your kindness is a new beginning,
Your pardon gratuitous bounty,
Your punishment justice,
Your decree a choice for the best!

If You bestow,
You stain not Your bestowal with obligation,
and if You withhold,
You withhold not in transgression.

You show gratitude to him who thanks You,
while You have inspired him to thank You.

You reward him who praises You,
while You have taught him Your praise.

You cover him whom,
if You willed,
You would expose,
and You are generous toward him from whom,
if You willed,
You would withhold.

Both are worthy of Your exposure and withholding,
but You have
founded Your acts upon gratuitous bounty,

channeled Your power into forbearance,
received him who disobeyed You with clemency,
and disregarded him who intended wrongdoing against himself.

You await their turning back without haste
and refrain from rushing them toward repentance,
so that the perisher among them may not perish
because of You
and the wretched may not be wretched
through Your favor,
but only after Your prolonged excusing him
and successive arguments against him,
as an act of generosity through Your pardon, O Generous,
and an act of kindliness through Your tenderness, O Clement!

It is You who has opened for Your servants
a door to Your pardon,
which You have named 'repentance'.
You have placed upon that door
a pointer from Your revelation,
lest they stray from it:
You have said (blessed are Your names),
Repent toward God with unswerving repentance!
It may be that Your Lord will acquit of your evil deeds
and will admit you into gardens
beneath which rivers flow,
upon the day when God will not degrade the Prophet
and those who have faith along with him,
their light running before them
and on their right hands,
and they say:

'Our Lord, complete for us our light, and forgive us!
Surely You are powerful over everything.'

What is the excuse

of him who remains heedless of entering that house
after the opening of the door
and the setting up of the pointer?

It is You who has raised the price against Yourself
to the advantage of Your servants,
desiring their profit in their trade with You,
their triumph through reaching You,
and their increase on account of You,
for You have said
(blessed is Your Name and high are You exalted),
Whoso brings a good deed
shall have ten the like of it,
and whoso brings an evil deed
shall only be recompensed the like of it.

You have said,
The likeness of those who expend their wealth
in the way of God
is as the likeness of a grain of corn
that sprouts seven ears,
in every ear a hundred grains;
so God multiplies unto whom He wills.

You have said,
Who is he that will lend to God a good loan,
and He will multiply it for him manifold?

And You have sent down in the Qur'an
similar verses on the multiplying of good deeds.

It is You who has pointed them
through Your speech from Your Unseen
and Your encouragement in which lies their good fortune
toward that which –

had You covered it from them –
their eyes would not have perceived,
their ears would not have heard,
and their imaginations would not have grasped,

for You have said,
Remember Me
and I will remember you
be thankful to Me,
and be you not thankless towards Me!

You have said,
If you are thankful,
surely I will increase you,
but if you are thankless, My
chastisement is surely terrible;

And You have said,
Supplicate Me
and I will respond to you,
surely those who wax too proud to worship Me
shall enter Gehenna utterly abject.

Hence You have named supplicating You 'worship'
and refraining from it 'waxing proud',
and You have threatened that the refraining from it
would yield entrance into Gehenna in utter abjection.

So they remember You for Your kindness,
they thank You for Your bounty,
they supplicate You by Your command,
and they donate for You
in order to seek Your increase;
in all this lies their deliverance from Your wrath
and their triumph through Your good pleasure.

Were any creature himself to direct another creature
to the like of that to which
You Yourself have directed Your servants,
he would be described by beneficence,
qualified by kindness,
and praised by every tongue.
So to You belongs praise
as long as there is found a way to praise You
and as long as there remains for praising
words by which You may be praised
and meanings which may be spent in praise!

O He who shows Himself praiseworthy to His servants
through beneficence and bounty,
flooding them with kindness and graciousness!
How much Your favor has been spread about among us,
Your kindness lavished upon us,
and Your goodness singled out for us!

You have guided us to
Your religion which You have chosen,
Your creed with which You are pleased,
and Your path which You have made smooth,
and You have shown us proximity to You
and arrival at Your generosity!

O God,
among the choicest of those duties
and the most special of those obligations
You have appointed the month of Ramadan,
which You have singled out from other months,
chosen from among all periods and eras,
and preferred over all times of the year
through the Qur'an and the Light
which You sent down within it,

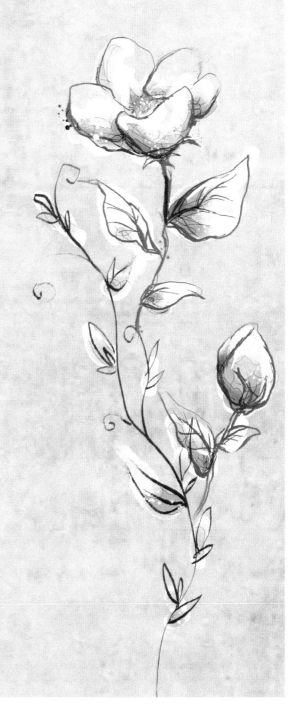

the faith
which You multiplied by means of it,
the fasting
which You obligated therein,
the standing in prayer
which You encouraged at its time,
and the Night of Decree
which You magnified therein,
the night which is better than a thousand months.

Through it You have preferred us
over the other communities
and through its excellence You have chosen us
to the exclusion of the people of the creeds.

We fasted by Your command in its daylight,
we stood in prayer with Your help in its night,
presenting ourselves by its fasting and its standing
to the mercy which You have held up before us,
and we found through it the means to Your reward.
And You are full of what is sought from You,
munificent with what is asked of Your bounty,
and near to him who strives for Your nearness.

This month stood among us
in a standing place of praise,
accompanied us
with the companionship of one approved,
and profited us
with the most excellent profit of the world's creatures.

Then it parted from us at
the completion of its time,
the end of its term,
and the fulfilment of its number.

So we bid farewell to it with the farewell of one
whose parting pains us,
whose leaving fills us with gloom and loneliness,
and to whom we have come to owe
a safeguarded claim,
an observed inviolability,
and a discharged right.

We say:
Peace be upon You,
O greatest month of God!
O festival of His friends!

Peace be upon You,
O most noble of accompanying times!
O best of months in days and hours!

Peace be upon You,
month in which
expectations come near
and good works are scattered about!

Peace be upon You,
comrade
who is great in worth when found
and who torments through absence when lost,
anticipated friend
whose parting gives pain!

Peace be upon You,
familiar
who brought comfort in coming,
thus making happy,
who left loneliness in going,
thus giving anguish!

Peace be upon You,
neighbor in whom
hearts became tender
and sins became few!

Peace be upon You,
helper who aided against Satan,
companion who made easy the paths of good-doing!

Peace be upon You -
How many became freedmen of God within You!
How happy those who observed the respect due to You!

Peace be upon You -
How many the sins You erased!
How many the kinds of faults You covered over!

Peace be upon You -
How drawn out were You for the sinners!
How awesome were You in the hearts of the faithful!

Peace be upon You,
month with which no days compete!

Peace be upon You,
month which is peace in all affairs!

Peace be upon You,
You whose companionship is not disliked,
You whose friendly mixing is not blamed!

Peace be upon You,

just as You have entered upon us with blessings
and cleansed us of the defilement of offenses!

Peace be upon You -
You are not bid farewell in annoyance
nor is Your fasting left in weariness!

Peace be upon You,
object of seeking before Your time,
object of sorrow before Your passing!

Peace be upon You -
How much evil was turned away from us through You!
How much good flowed upon us because of You!

Peace be upon You
and upon the Night of Decree
which is better than a thousand months!

Peace be upon You -
How much we craved You yesterday!
How intensely we shall yearn for You tomorrow!

Peace be upon You
and upon Your bounty
which has now been made unlawful to us
and upon Your blessings gone by
which have now been stripped away from us!

O God,
we are the people of this month.
Through it You have ennobled us
and given us success

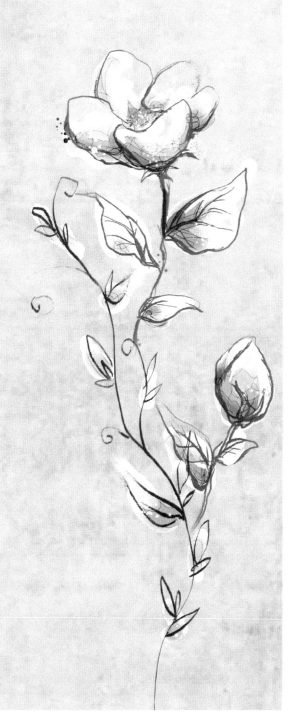

because of Your kindness,
while the wretched are ignorant of its time.
Made unlawful to them is its bounty
because of their wretchedness.

You are the patron of the knowledge of it
by which You have preferred us,
and its prescribed practices to which You have guided us.
We have undertaken, through Your giving success,
its fasting and its standing in prayer,
but with shortcomings,
and we have performed little of much.

O God, so to You belongs praise,
in admission of evil doing
and confession of negligence,
and to You belongs
remorse firmly knitted in our hearts
and seeking of pardon sincerely uttered by our tongues.

Reward us,
in spite of the neglect that befell us in this month,
with a reward through which
we may reach the bounty desired from it
and win the varieties of its craved stores!

Make incumbent upon us Your pardon
for our falling short of Your right in this month
and make our lives which lie before us
reach the coming month of Ramadan!
Once You have made us reach it,
help us perform the worship of which You are worthy,
cause us to undertake the obedience which You deserve,
and grant us righteous works
that we may fulfil Your right
in these two months of the months of time.

O God, as for the small and large sins
which we have committed in this our month,
the misdeeds into which we have fallen,
and the offenses which we have earned
purposefully or in forgetfulness,
wronging ourselves thereby
or violating the respect due to others,
bless Muhammad and his Household,
cover us over with Your covering,
pardon us through Your pardoning,
place us not before the eyes of the gloaters because of that,
stretch not toward us the tongues of the defamers,
and employ us in that which will alleviate and expiate
whatever You disapprove from us within it
through Your clemency which does not run out,
and Your bounty which does not diminish!

O God, bless Muhammad and his Household,
redress our being afflicted by our month,
bless us in this day of our festival and our fast-breaking,
make it one of the best of days that have passed over us,
the greatest in attracting Your pardon,
and the most effacing toward sins,
and forgive us our sins, both the concealed and the public!

O God, with the passing of this month
make us pass forth from our offenses,
with its departure
make us depart from our evil deeds,
and appoint us thereby among its most felicitous people,
the most plentiful of them in portion,
and the fullest of them in share!

O God, when any person observes this month as it should be observed,
safeguards its inviolability as it should be safeguarded,

attends to its bounds as they should be attended to,
fears its misdeeds as they should be feared,
or seeks nearness to You with any act of nearness-seeking
which
makes incumbent upon him Your good pleasure
and bends toward him Your mercy,
give to us the like [of that] from Your wealth and
bestow it upon us in multiples through Your bounty, for
Your bounty does not diminish,
Your treasuries do not decrease but overflow,
the mines of Your beneficence are not exhausted,
and Your bestowal is the bestowal full of delight!

O God, bless Muhammad and his Household
and write for us the like of the wages
of him who fasted in it
or worshipped You within it
until the Day of Resurrection!

O God, we repent to You in our day of fast-breaking,
which You have appointed
for the faithful
a festival and a joy
and for the people of Your creed
a time of assembly and gathering,
from every misdeed we did,
ill work we sent ahead,
or evil thought we secretly conceived,
the repentance of one who does not harbor a return to sin
and who afterwards will not go back to offense,
an unswerving repentance rid of doubt and wavering.
So accept it from us,
be pleased with us,
and fix us within it!

O God,
provide us with fear of the threatened punishment

and yearning for the promised reward,
so that we may find
the pleasure of that for which we supplicate You
and the sorrow of that from which we seek sanctuary in You!

And place us with You among the repenters,
those upon whom You have made Your love obligatory
and from whom You have accepted
the return to obeying You!
O Most Just of the just!

O God,
show forbearance toward our fathers and our mothers
and all the people of our religion,
those who have gone and those who will pass by,
until the Day of Resurrection!

O God,
bless our prophet Muhammad and his Household,
as You have blessed Your angels brought nigh,
bless him and his Household,
as You have blessed Your prophets sent out,
bless him and his Household,
as You have blessed Your righteous servants –
and better than that, O Lord of the worlds! –
a blessing whose benediction will reach us,
whose benefit will attain to us,
and through which our supplication may be granted!
You are the most generous of those who are beseeched,
the most sufficient of those in whom confidence is had,
the most bestowing of those from whom bounty is asked,
and You are powerful over everything!

S46 - His Supplication on the Day of Fast-Breaking and on Friday

When he finished his prayer, He would stand in place, face the *qibla*, and say:

O He who has mercy upon him toward whom the servants show no mercy!
O He who accepts him whom the cities will not accept!
O He who looks not down upon those who have need of Him!

O He who disappoints not those who implore Him!
O He who slaps not the brow of the people of boldness toward Him
with rejection!

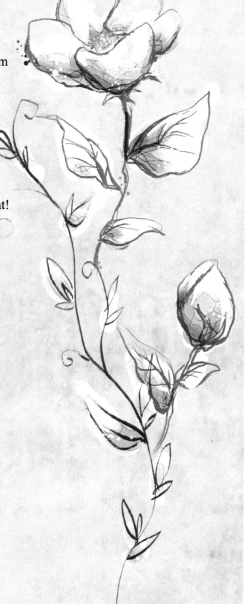

O He who collects the little that is given to Him
and shows gratitude for the paltry that is done for Him!

O He who shows gratitude for the small and rewards with the great!
O He who comes close to him who comes close to Him!

O He who invites to Himself him who turns his back on Him!
O He who changes not favor and rushes not to vengeance!

O He who causes the good deed to bear fruit
so that He may make it grow,
and overlooks the evil deed
so that He may efface it!

Hopes turn back with needs fulfilled
short of the extent of Your generosity,
the cups of requests fill up
with the overflow of Your munificence,
and attributes fall apart
without reaching Your description.

For to You belongs the highest highness
above everything high,
and the most glorious majesty
beyond every majesty!

Everything majestic before You is small,
everything eminent beside Your eminence vile!
Those who reach other than You are disappointed,
those who present themselves to other than You
have lost,
those who stay with other than You
have perished,
and those who retreat –
except those who retreat to Your bounty –
are desolate!

Your door is open to the beseechers,
Your munificence free to the askers,
Your help near to the help-seekers!

The expectant are not disappointed by You,
those who present themselves
despair not of Your bestowal,
the forgiveness-seekers
become not wretched through Your vengeance!

Your provision is spread among those who disobey You,
Your clemency presents itself to those hostile toward You,
Your habit is beneficence toward the evildoers,
and Your wont is to spare the transgressors,
so much so that Your lack of haste deludes them from returning,
and Your disregard bars them from desisting!

You act without haste toward them
so that they will come back to Your command

and You disregard them
confident in the permanence of Your kingdom,
so You seal him who is worthy of it with felicity,
and You abandon him who is worthy of it to wretchedness!

All of them come home to Your decree,
their affairs revert to Your command;
Your authority grows not feeble through their drawn out term,
Your proof is not refuted by the failure to hurry after them.

Your argument is established, never refuted,
Your authority fixed, never removed.
Permanent woe belongs
to him who inclines away from You,
forsaking disappointment
to him who is disappointed by You,
and the most wretched wretchedness
to him who is deluded about You!

How much he will move about in Your chastisement!
How long he will frequent Your punishment!
How far his utmost end from relief!
How he will despair of an easy exit!
[All of this] as justice from Your decree
(You are not unjust in it!),
and equity from Your judgement
(You do not act wrongfully against him!).

You supported the arguments,
tested the excuses,
began with threats,
showed gentleness with encouragement,
struck similitudes,
made long the respite,
delayed,
while You are able to hurry,

and acted without haste,
while You are full of quick accomplishment!

Not because of
incapacity is Your slowness,
feebleness Your giving respite,
heedlessness Your showing restraint,
dissemblance Your waiting!
But that Your argument be more conclusive,
Your generosity more perfect,
Your beneficence more exhaustive,
Your favor more complete!
All of this has been and always was,
is and ever will be.

Your argument is greater
than that its totality be described,
Your glory more elevated
than that it be limited in its core,
Your favor more abundant
than that its entirety be counted,
Your beneficence more abundant
than that thanks be given for its least amount!

Speechlessness has made me fall short of praising You,
restraint has made me powerless to glorify You,
and the most I can do is admit to inability,
not out of desire, my God,
but out of incapacity.

So here I am:
I repair to You by coming forward,
and I ask from You good support
So bless Muhammad and his Household,
hear my whispered words,
grant my supplication,

seal not my day with disappointment,
slap not my brow by rejecting my request,
and make noble my coming from You
and my going back to You!

Surely You are not constrained by what You desire,
nor incapable of what You are asked!
You are powerful over everything,
and 'There is no force and no strength save in God,
the All-high, the All-mighty!'

S47 - His Supplication on the Day of 'Arafa

Praise belongs to God, Lord of the worlds!

O God,
to You belongs praise!
Originator of the heavens and the earth!
Possessor of majesty and munificence!
Lord of lords!
Object of worship of every worshiper!
Creator of every creature!
Inheritor of all things!
There is nothing like Him,
knowledge of nothing escapes Him,
He encompasses everything, and He is
watchful over everything.

You are God,
there is no god but You,
the Unique, the Alone,
the Single, the Isolated.

You are God,
there is no god but You,
the Generous, the Generously Bestowing,
the All-mighty, the Mightily Exalted,
the Magnificent, the Magnificently Magnified.

You are God,
there is no god but You,
the All-high, the Sublimely High,
the Strong in prowess.

You are God,

there is no god but You,
the All-merciful, the All-compassionate,
the All-knowing, the All-wise.

You are God,
there is no god but You,
the All-hearing, the All-seeing,
the Eternal, the All-aware.

You are God,
there is no god but You,
the Generous, the Most Generous,
the Everlasting, the Most Everlasting.

You are God,
there is no god but You,
the First before every one,
the Last after every number.

You are God,
there is no god but You,
the Close in His highness,
the High in His closeness.

You are God,
there is no god but You,
Possessor of radiance and glory,
magnificence and praise.

You are God,
there is no god but You.
You have brought forth the things without root,
formed what You have formed without exemplar,
and originated the originated things without limitation.

It is You
who have ordained each thing with an ordination,
eased each thing with an easing,
and governed everything below Yourself with a governing.

It is You
whom no associate helps with Your creation
and no vizier aids in Your command.
You have no witness and no equal.

It is You
who willed,
and what You willed was unfailing,
who decreed,
and what You decreed was just,
who decided,
and what You decided was fair.

It is You
whom place does not contain,
before whose authority no authority stands up,
and whom no proof or explication can thwart.

It is You
who have counted everything in numbers,
appointed for everything a term,and ordained
everything with an ordination.

It is You
before whose selfness imaginations fall short,
before whose how-ness understandings have no capacity,
and the place of whose where-ness eyes perceive not.

174

It is You
who have no bounds,
lest You be bounded,
who are not exemplified,
lest You be found,
who do not beget,
lest You be begotten.

It is You
with whom there is no opposite,
lest it contend with You,
who have no equal,
lest it vie with You,
who have no rival,
lest it resist You.

It is You
who are He who began, devised,
brought forth, originated,
and made well all that He made.

Glory be to You!
How majestic is Your station!
How high Your place among the places!
How cleanly Your Separator cleaves with the truth!

Glory be to You!
The Gentle - how gentle You are!
The Clement - how clement You are!
The Wise - how knowing You are!

Glory be to You!
The King - how invincible You are!
The Munificent - how full of plenty You are!

The Elevated - how elevated You are!
Possessor of radiance and glory,
magnificence and praise!

Glory be to You!
You have stretched forth Your hand with good things,
and from You guidance has come to be known,
so he who begs from You religion or this world
will find You.

Glory be to You!
Whatever passes in Your knowledge is subjected to You,
all below Your Throne are humbled before Your mightiness,
and every one of Your creatures follows You in submission.

Glory be to You!
You are not sensed, nor touched,
nor felt, nor beguiled,
nor held back, nor challenged,
nor kept up with, nor resisted,
nor deceived, nor circumvented.

Glory be to You!
Your path is smooth ground,
Your command right guidance,
and You are a living, eternal refuge.

Glory be to You!
Your word is decisive,
Your decree unfailing,
Your will resolute.

Glory be to You!
None can reject Your wish,

none can change Your words.

Glory be to You,
Bedazzling in signs,
Creator of the heavens,
Author of the spirits!

To You belongs praise,
a praise that will be permanent with Your permanence!

To You belongs praise,
a praise everlasting through Your favor!

To You belongs praise,
a praise that will parallel Your benefaction!

To You belongs praise,
a praise that will increase Your good pleasure!

To You belongs praise,
a praise along with the praise of every praiser
and a thanksgiving before which falls short
the thanksgiving of every thanksgiver;

a praise which is suitable for none but You
and through which nearness is sought to none but You;

a praise which will make permanent the first [bounty]
and call forth the permanence of the last;

a praise which will multiply through recurrence of times

and increase through successive doublings;

a praise which the guardians will not be able to number
and which exceeds what the writers number in Your Book;

a praise which will counter balance Your glorious
Throne and equal Your elevated Footstool;
a praise whose reward with You will be complete
and whose recompense will comprise every recompense;

a praise whose outward conforms to its inward,
and whose inward conforms to correct intention;

a praise with whose like no creature has praised You
and whose excellence none knows but You;

a praise in which he who strives to multiply Your praise
will be helped
and he who draws the bow to the utmost in fulfilling it
will be confirmed;

a praise which will
gather all the praise which You have created
and tie together all which You will afterwards create;

a praise than which no praise is nearer to Your word
and than which none is greater from any who praise You;

a praise whose fullness will obligate increase
through Your generosity
and to which You will join increase after increase
as graciousness from You;

a praise that will befit the generosity of Your face
and meet the might of Your majesty!

My Lord,
bless Muhammad and the Household of Muhammad,
the distinguished, the chosen,
the honored, the brought nigh,
with the most excellent of Your blessings,
benedict him
with the most complete of Your benedictions,
and have mercy upon him
with the most enjoyable of Your mercies!

My Lord,
bless Muhammad and his Household
with a fruitful blessing,
more fruitful than which there is no blessing!
Bless him
with a growing blessing,
more growing than which there is no blessing!
And bless him
with a pleasing blessing,
beyond which there is no blessing!

My Lord,
bless Muhammad and his Household
with a blessing
which will please him
and increase his good pleasure!
Bless him
with a blessing
which will please You
and increase Your good pleasure toward him!
And bless him
with a blessing

through other than which You will not be pleased for him,
and for which You see no one else worthy!

My Lord,
bless Muhammad and his Household
with a blessing which will
pass beyond Your good pleasure,
be continuous in its continuity
through Your subsistence,
and never be spent,
just as Your words will never be spent!

My Lord,
bless Muhammad and his Household
with a blessing which will
tie together the blessings of
Your angels, Your prophets, Your messengers,
and those who obey You,
comprise the blessings of Your servants,
jinn or mankind,
and those worthy of Your response,
and bring together the blessings
of every one of the kinds of Your creatures
which You have sown and authored!

My Lord,
bless Muhammad and his Household
with a blessing
which will encompass every blessing,
bygone and new!
Bless him and his Household
with a blessing which
is pleasing to You
and everyone below You
and will bring forth with all that
a blessing
with which You will multiply those blessings

and increase them through the recurrence of days
with an increasing in multiples
which none can count but You!

My Lord,
bless the best of his Household,
those whom You have
chosen for Your command,
appointed the treasurers of Your knowledge,
the guardians of Your religion,
Your vicegerents in Your earth,
and Your arguments against Your servants,
purified from uncleanness and defilement
through a purification by Your desire,
and made the mediation to You
and the road to Your Garden!

My Lord,
bless Muhammad and his Household
with a blessing which
makes plentiful Your gifts and generosity,
perfects for them Your bestowals and awards,
and fills out their share of Your kindly acts and benefits!

My Lord,
bless him and his Household
with a blessing
whose first has no term,
whose term has no limit,
and whose last has no utmost end!

My Lord,
bless them to
the weight of Your Throne and all below it,
the amount that fills the heavens and all above them,
the number of Your earths and all below and between them,

a blessing that will bring them near to You in proximity,
please You and them,
and be joined to its likes forever!

O God,
surely You have confirmed Your religion in all times
with an Imam whom You have set up
as a guidepost to Your servants
and a lighthouse in Your lands,
after his cord has been joined to Your cord!
You have appointed him the means to Your good pleasure,
made obeying him obligatory,
cautioned against disobeying him,
and commanded
following his commands,
abandoning his prohibitions,
and that no forward-goer go ahead of him or back-keeper
keep back from him!
So he is the preservation of the shelter-seekers,
the cave of the faithful,
the handhold of the adherents,
and the radiance of the worlds!

O God,
so inspire Your guardian to give thanks
for that in which You have favored him,
inspire us with the like concerning him,
grant him an authority from You to help him,
open for him an easy opening,
aid him with Your mightiest pillar,
brace up his back,
strengthen his arm,
guard him with Your eye,
defend him with Your safeguarding,
help him with Your angels,
and assist him with Your most victorious troops!

Through him
establish Your Book, Your bounds, Your laws,
and the norms of Your Messenger's Sunna
(Your blessings, O God,
be upon him and his Household),
bring to life the guideposts of Your religion,
deadened by the wrongdoers,
burnish the rust of injustice from Your way,
sift the adversity from Your road,
eliminate those who deviate from Your path,
and erase those who seek crookedness in Your straightness!

Make his side mild toward Your friends,
stretch forth his hand over Your enemies,
give us
his clemency, his mercy,
his tenderness, his sympathy,
and make us
his hearers and obeyers,
strivers toward his good pleasure,
assistants in helping him and defending him,
and brought near through that to You
and Your Messenger
(Your blessings, O God,
be upon him and his Household).

O God,
and bless
the friends [of the Imams], the
confessors of their station, the
keepersto their course, the pursuers
of theirtracks, the clingers to their
handhold, the adherents to their
guardianship, the followers of their
imamate, the submitters to their
command, the strivers to obey them,
the awaiters of their days,

the directors of their eyes toward them,
with blessings blessed, pure, growing,
fresh, and fragrant!

Give them and their spirits peace,
bring together their affair in reverential fear,
set right their situations,
turn toward them,
Surely You are Ever-turning, All-compassionate
and the Best of forgivers,
and place us with them in the Abode of Peace,
through Your mercy,
O Most Merciful of the merciful!

O God,
this is the Day of 'Arafa,
a day which You have made noble, given honor, and magnified.
Within it You have spread Your mercy,
showed kindness through Your pardon,
and made plentiful Your giving,
and by it You have been bounteous toward Your servants.

I am Your servant whom You favored before creating him
and after creating him.
You made him one of those whom You
guided to Your religion,
gave success in fulfilling Your right,
preserved through Your cord,
included within Your party,
and directed aright to befriend Your friends
and show enmity to Your enemies.

Then You commanded him,
but he did not follow Your commands,
You restricted Him,
but he did not heed Your restrictions,

You prohibited him from disobedience toward You,
but he broke Your command by doing what You had prohibited,
not in contention with You,
nor to display pride toward You;
on the contrary, his caprice called him
to that which You had set apart and cautioned against,
and he was helped in that by Your enemy and his enemy.
So he went ahead with it
knowing Your threat,
hoping for Your pardon,
and relying upon Your forbearance,
though he was the most obligated of Your servants –
given Your kindness toward him –
not to do so.

Here I am, then, before You,
despised, lowly, humble, abject, fearful,
confessing the dreadful sins with which I am burdened
and the great offenses that I have committed,
seeking sanctuary in Your forgiveness,
asking shelter in Your mercy,
and certain that
no sanctuary-giver will give me sanctuary from You
and no withholder will hold me back from You.

So act kindly toward me,
just as You act kindly
by Your shielding him who commits sins,
be munificent toward me,
just as You are munificent
by pardoning him who throws himself before You,
and show kindness to me,
just as it is nothing great for You to show kindness
by forgiving him who expectantly hopes in You!

Appoint for me in this day an allotment
through which I may attain

a share of Your good pleasure,
and send me not back destitute
of that with which Your worshipers return
from among Your servants!

Though I have not forwarded
the righteous deeds
which they have forwarded,
I have forwarded the profession of Your Unity
and the negation from You
of opposites, rivals, and likenesses,
I have come to You by the gateways
by which You have commanded
that people come,
and I have sought nearness to You
through that without seeking nearness through which
none gains nearness to You.

Then I followed all this
with repeated turning toward You,
lowliness and abasement before You,
opinion of You,
and trust in what is with You;
and to that I coupled hope in You,
since the one who hopes in You
is seldom disappointed!

I asked You with the asking of one
vile, lowly,
pitiful, poor,
fearful, seeking sanctuary;
all that in fear and pleading
seeking refuge and asking shelter,
not presumptuous through the pride of the proud,
nor exalting myself with the boldness of the obedient,
nor presumptuous of the intercession of the interceders.

For I am still the least of the least
and the lowliest of the lowly,
like a dust mote or less!
O He who does not hurry the evildoersnor restrain those
living in ease!
O He who shows kindness through releasing the stumblers
and gratuitous bounty through respiting the offenders!

I am the evildoer, the confessor, the offender, the stumbler!
I am he who was audacious toward You as one insolent!
I am he who disobeyed You with forethought!

I am he who hid myself from Your servants
and blatantly showed myself to You!

I am he who was awed by Your servants
and felt secure from You!

I am he who dreaded not Your penalty
and feared not Your severity!

I am the offender against himself!
I am the hostage to his own affliction!
I am short in shame!
I am long in suffering!

By the right of him whom You have distinguished
among Your creation
and by him whom You have chosen
for Yourself!
By the right of him whom You have selected
from among Your creatures
and by him whom You have picked

for Your task!
By the right of him the obeying of whom You have joined
to obeying You,
and by him the disobeying of whom You have made
like disobeying You!
And by the right of him whose friendship You have bound
to Your friendship
and by him whose enmity You have linked
to Your enmity!
Shield me in this day of mine,
by that through which You shield
him who prays fervently to You
while disavowing
and him who seeks refuge in Your forgiveness
while repenting!

Attend to me
with that through which You attend to the people of
obedience toward You,
proximity to You,
and rank with You!

Single me out,
as You single him out who
fulfils Your covenant,
fatigues himself for Your sake alone,
and exerts himself in Your good pleasure!

Take me not to task for
my neglect in respect to You,
my transgressing the limit in Your bounds,
and stepping outside Your ordinances!

Draw me not on little by little by granting me a respite,
like the drawing on little by little
of him who withholds from me the good he has

by not sharing with You in letting favor down upon me!

Arouse me from
the sleep of the heedless,
the slumber of the prodigal,
and the dozing of the forsaken!

Take my heart to that in which You have
employed the devout,
enthralled the worshipers,
and rescued the remiss!

Give me refuge from that which will
keep me far from You,
come between me and my share from You,
and bar me from that which I strive for in You!

Make easy for me
the road of good deeds toward You,
racing to them from where You have commanded,
and coveting them as You desire!

Efface me not along with
those whom You efface
for thinking lightly of what You have promised!

Destroy me not with
those whom You destroy
for exposing themselves to Your hate!

Annihilate me not among
those whom You annihilate
for deviating from Your roads!

Deliver me from the floods of trial,
save me from the gullets of affliction,
and grant me sanctuary from being seized by respite!

Come between me and the enemy who misguides me,
the caprice which ruins me,
and the failing which overcomes me!

Turn not away from me
with the turning away in wrath
from one with whom You are not pleased!

Let me not lose heart in expecting from You,
lest I be overcome by despair of Your mercy!

Grant me not that which I cannot endure,
lest You weigh me down
with the surplus of Your love which You load upon me!

Send me not from Your hand,
the sending of him who possesses no good,
toward whom You have no need,
and who turns not back [to You]!

Cast me not with the casting of him who has
fallen from the eye of Your regard
and been wrapped in degradation from You!
Rather take my hand [and save me] from
the falling of the stumblers,
the disquiet of the deviators,
the slip of those deluded,
and the plight of the perishers!

Release me from that with which You have afflicted
the ranks of Your servants and handmaids
and make me reach the utmost degrees of him
about whom You are concerned,
towards whom You show favor,
and with whom You are pleased,
so that You let him live as one praiseworthy
and take him to You as one felicitous!

Collar me with the collar of abstaining from that which
makes good deeds fail
and takes away blessings!

Impart to my heart restraint before
ugly works of evil
and disgraceful misdeeds!

Divert me not
by that which I cannot reach except through You
from doing that which alone makes You pleased with me!

Root out from my heart the love of this vile world,
which keeps from everything which is with You,
bars from seeking the mediation to You,
and distracts from striving for nearness to You!

Embellish for me solitude
in prayer whispered to You
by night and by day!

Give me a preservation which will
bring me close to dread of You,

cut me off from committing things made unlawful by You,
and spare me from captivation by dreadful sins!

Give me purification from the defilement of disobedience,
take away from me the filth of offenses,
dress me in the dress of Your well-being,
cloak me in the cloak of Your release,
wrap me in Your ample favors,
and clothe me in Your bounty and Your graciousness!

Strengthen me with Your giving success
and Your pointing the right way,
help me toward righteous intention,
pleasing words,
and approved works,
and entrust me not to my force and my strength
in place of Your force and Your strength!

Degrade me not on the day You raise me up to meet You,
disgrace me not before Your friends,
make me not forget remembering You,
take not away from me thanking You,
but enjoin it upon me in states of inattention
when the ignorant are heedless of Your boons,
and inspire me to
laud what You have done for me
and confess to what You have conferred upon me!

Place my beseeching You above the beseeching of the beseechers
and my praise of You above the praise of the praisers!

Abandon me not with my neediness for You,
destroy me not for what I have done for You,
and slap not my brow with that with which You
slap the brow of those who contend with You,

for I am submitted to You.
I know
that the argument is Yours,
that You are closest to bounty,most
accustomed to beneficence,worthy of
reverent fear,and worthy of forgiveness,
that You are closer to pardoning than to
punishing,
and that You are nearer to covering over
than to making notorious!

Let me live an agreeable life
that will tie together what I want
and reach what I love
while I not bring what You dislike
and not commit what You have prohibited;
and make me die the death of him
whose light runs before him and on his right hand!

Abase me before Yourself
and exalt me before Your creatures,
lower me when I am alone with You
and raise me among Your servants,
free me from need for him who has no need of me
and increase me in neediness and poverty toward You!

Give me refuge from
the gloating of enemies,
the arrival of affliction,
lowliness and suffering!
Shield me in what You see from me,
the shielding of him who
would have power over violence
had he no clemency,
and would seize for misdeeds
had he no lack of haste!

When You desire for a people a trial or an evil,
deliver me from it,
for I seek Your shelter;
and since You have not stood me in the station of disgrace
in this world of Yours,
stand me not in such a station
in the next world of Yours!

Couple for me the beginnings of Your kindnesses with their ends
and the ancient of Your benefits with the freshly risen!
Prolong not my term with a prolonging through which my heart
will harden!
Strike me not with a striking
that will take away my radiance!
Visit me not with
a meanness that will diminish my worth
or a decency that will keep my rank unknown!

Frighten me not
with a fright by which I will despair
or a terror through which I will dread,
but make me
stand in awe of Your threat,
take precautions against Your leaving no excuses
and Your warning,
and tremble at the recitation of Your verses!

Fill my night with life by keeping me awake therein for
worshipping You,
solitude with vigil for You,
exclusive devotion to reliance upon You,
setting my needs before You,
and imploring that You will
set my neck free from the Fire
and grant me sanctuary from Your chastisement,

within which its inhabitants dwell!

Leave me not
blindly wandering in my insolence
or inattentive in my perplexity for a time,
make me not
an admonition to him who takes admonishment,
a punishment exemplary for him who takes heed,
a trial for him who observes,
devise not against me along with those against whom You devise,
replace me not with another, change not my name,
transform not my body,
appoint me not
a mockery for Your creatures,
a laughing-stock for Yourself,
a follower of anything but Your good pleasure,
a menial servant for anything but avenging You!

Let me find
the coolness of Your pardon
and the sweetness of
Your mercy,
Your repose,
Your ease,
and the garden of Your bliss!
Let me taste,
through some of Your boundless plenty,
the flavor of
being free for what You love
and striving in what brings about proximity
with You and to You,
and give me a gift from among Your gifts!

Make my commerce profitable
and my return without loss, fill me
with fear of Your station,

make me yearn for the meeting with You,
and allow me to repent with an unswerving repentance
along with which You let no sins remain,
small or large,
and leave no wrongs, open or secret!

Root out rancor toward the faithful from my breast,
bend my heart toward the humble,
be toward me as You are toward the righteous,
adorn me with the adornment of the Godfearing,
appoint for me
a goodly report among those yet to come
and a growing remembrance among the later folk,and
take me to the plain of those who came first!

Complete the lavishness of Your favor upon me,
clothe me in its repeated generosities,
fill my hand with Your benefits,
drive Your generous gifts to me,
make me the neighbor of the best of Your friends
in the Gardens which You have adorned for Your chosen,
and wrap me in Your noble presents
in the stations prepared for Your beloveds!

Appoint for me
a resting place with You
where I may seek haven in serenity,
and a resort to which I may revert
and rest my eyes,
weigh not against me my dreadful misdeeds,
destroy me not on the day the secrets are tried,
eliminate from me every doubt and uncertainty,
appoint for me a way in the truth from every mercy,
make plentiful for me the portions of gifts
from Your granting of awards,
and fill out for me the shares of beneficence
from Your bestowal of bounty!

Make my heart trust in what is with You
and my concern free for what is Yours,
employ me in that in which You employ Your pure friends,
drench my heart with Your obedience when intellects are distracted,
and combine within me
independence, continence,
ease, release,
health, plenty,
tranquility, and well-being!

Make not fail
my good deeds
through my disobedience that stains them
or my private times of worship
through the instigations of Your trial!
Safeguard my face from asking
from anyone in the world,
and drive me far from begging
for that which is with the ungodly!

Make me not an aid to the wrongdoers,
nor their hand and helper in erasing Your Book!
Defend me whence I know not with a defense
through which You protect me!
Open toward me the gates of Your repentance, Your mercy,
Your clemency, and Your boundless provision!
Surely I am one of those who beseech You!
And complete Your favor toward me!
Surely You are the best of those who show favor!

Place the rest of my life in the hajj and the 'umrah
seeking Your face,
O Lord of the worlds!
And may God bless Muhammad and his Household, the good, the pure, and peace be upon him
and them always and forever!

S48 - His Supplication on the Day of Sacrifice (Eid al-Adh-ha) and on Friday

O God,
this is a blessed and fortunate day,
within which the Muslims are gathered
in the quarters of Your earth.
Among them are present the asker, the seeker,
the beseecher, the fearful,
while You are looking upon their needs.
So I ask You by Your munificence and generosity
and easy upon You is what I ask You! -
that You bless Muhammad and his Household.

And I ask You, O God, our Lord -
for Yours is the kingdom and Yours is the praise;
there is no god but You,
the Clement, the Generous,
the All-loving, the All-kind,
Possessor of majesty and munificence,
Originator of the heavens and the earth -
whenever You apportion among Your faithful servants
good, well-being,
blessing, guidance,
works in obedience to You,
or good through which
You are kind to them by guiding them to You,
or raise them up a degree with You,
or give them the good of this world or the next,
that You give me amply my share and allotment of it.

And I ask You, O God -
for Yours is the kingdom and the praise;
there is no god but You -
that You bless Muhammad,
Your servant and Your messenger,

Your beloved and Your selected friend,
Your chosen from among Your creation,
and the Household of Muhammad,
the pious, the pure, the chosen,
with a blessing no one has strength to count but You,
that You associate us with
the most righteous of Your faithful servants
who supplicate You today –
O Lord of the worlds!—
and that You forgive us and them!
Surely You are powerful over everything.

O God,
toward You I aim with my need
and before You I set my poverty, my neediness, my misery,
for I have more trust in Your forgiveness and Your mercy
than in my own works.
Your forgiveness and Your mercy are vaster than my sins.
So bless Muhammad and the Household of Muhammad,
and attend to the accomplishment of every need of mine through
Your power over it,
its easiness for You,
my poverty toward You,
and Your freedom from need for me!
I will come upon no good whatsoever unless through You,
no one other than You will turn any evil away from me,
and I have hope in none but You for my affair
in the next world and in this world.

O God,
if anyone has ever
arranged,
made ready,
prepared,
and drawn himself up
to be received by a creature
in hope of his support and awards,
then today toward You, my Master, is

my arrangement,
my making ready,
my preparation,
and my drawing up,
in hope of Your pardon and support
and in seeking to attain to You and Your prize.

O God,
so bless Muhammad and the Household of Muhammad
and disappoint not my hope in that today!
O He who is not troubled by those who ask
and diminished by those who attain their desire!
I come not before You trusting
in a righteous work I have sent ahead,
nor in the intercession of any creature in whom
I have hope,
except the intercession of Muhammad
and the Folk of his House
(upon him and upon them be Your peace).

I come to You admitting sin and evildoing toward myself.
I come to You hoping for Your abounding pardon
through which You have pardoned the offenders,
while their long persistence in dreadful sin
did not prevent You
from returning toward them with mercy and forgiveness!

O He whose mercy is wide
and whose pardon is abounding!
O All-mighty!
O All-mighty!
O All-generous!
O All-generous!
Bless Muhammad and the Household of Muhammad,
return toward me through Your mercy,
be tender toward me through Your bounty,
and spread out Your forgiveness upon me!

O God,
this station belongs to Your vicegerents, Your chosen,
while the places of Your trusted ones
in the elevated degree which You have singled out for them
have been forcibly stripped!
But You are the Ordainer of that -
Your command is not overcome,
the inevitable in Your governing is not overstepped!
However You will and whenever You will!
In that which You know best,
You are not accused for Your creation or Your will!
Then Your selected friends, Your vicegerents,
were overcome, vanquished, forcibly stripped;
they see Your decree replaced,
Your Book discarded,
Your obligations distorted from the aims of Your laws,
and the Sunna of Your Prophet abandoned!

O God,
curse their enemies among those of old and the later folk,
and all those pleased with their acts,
and their adherents and followers!

O God,
bless Muhammad and the Household of Muhammad
(surely You are All-laudable, All-glorious)
like Your blessing, benedictions, and salutations
upon Your chosen Abraham and the people of Abraham!
And hasten for them relief,
ease,
help,
strengthening,
and confirmation!

O God,

and make me
one of the people who profess Your Unity,
have faith in You,
and attest to Your Messenger
and the Imams toward whom You have enjoined obedience,
and one of those through whom and at whose hands
this takes place!
Amen, Lord of the worlds!

O God,
nothing repels Your wrath but Your clemency,
nothing repels Your displeasure but Your pardon,
nothing grants sanctuary from Your punishment but Your mercy,
and nothing will deliver me from You
except pleading to You before You,
so bless Muhammad and the Household of Muhammad,
and give us on Your part, my God,
relief by means of the power
through which You bring the dead servants to life
and revive the dead lands.

Destroy me not through gloom, my God,
before You respond to me
and give me the knowledge of Your response to
my supplication!
Let me taste the flavor of well-being to the end of my term!
And let not my enemy gloat over me,
place not my neck in his power,
and give him not authority over me!

My God,
if You raise me up,
who is there to push me down?
If You push me down,
who is there to raise me up?
If You honor me,
who is there to humiliate me?

If You humiliate me,
who is there to honor me?
If You chastise me,
who is there to have mercy upon me?
If You destroy me,
who is there to stand up for Your servant against You
or ask You about his affair?
But I know that there is no wrong in Your decree
and no hurry in Your vengeance.
He alone hurries who fears to miss,
and only the weak needs to wrong.
But You are exalted, my God,
high indeed above all that!

O God,
bless Muhammad and the Household of Muhammad,
make me not the target of affliction
nor the object of Your vengeance,
respite me,
comfort me,
release me from my stumble,
and afflict me not with an affliction
in the wake of an affliction,
for You have seen my frailty,
the paucity of my stratagems,
and my pleading to You!

I seek refuge in You today, my God, from Your wrath,
so bless Muhammad and his Household
and give me refuge!

I seek sanctuary in You today from Your displeasure,
so bless Muhammad and his Household,
and give me sanctuary!

I ask You security from Your chastisement,
so bless Muhammad and his Household,

and give me security!

I seek guidance from You,
so bless Muhammad and his Household
and guide me!

I seek help from You,
so bless Muhammad and his Household
and help me!

I ask You for mercy,
so bless Muhammad and his Household
and have mercy upon me!

I seek sufficiency from You,
so bless Muhammad and his Household
and suffice me!

I seek provision from You,
so bless Muhammad and his Household
and provide for me!

I seek assistance from You,
so bless Muhammad and his Household
and assist me!

I pray forgiveness for my past sins,
so bless Muhammad and his Household
and forgive me!

I ask You to preserve me from sin,
so bless Muhammad and his Household

and preserve me,
for I will not return to anything You dislike from me,
if You will that!

My Lord!
My Lord!
O All-loving!
O All-kind!
O Possessor of majesty and munificence!
Bless Muhammad and his Household,
and grant me everything that I
ask from You,
seek from You,
and beseech from You!
Will it, ordain it, decree it, and accomplish it!
Give me good in that of it which You decree!
Bless me in that,
be gratuitously bountiful toward me through it,
make me happy in that of it which You give to me,
and increase me in Your bounty
and the plenty of what is with You,
for You are Boundless, Generous!
And link that to the good and the bliss of the next world,
O Most Merciful of the merciful!

S49 - His Supplication in Repelling Enemies

His Supplication in Repelling the Trickery of Enemies and Driving away their Severity

My God,
You guided me
but I diverted myself,
You admonished me
but my heart became hardened,
You tried me graciously
but I disobeyed.
Then, when You caused me to know it,
I came to know that from which You had turned
[me] away,
so I prayed forgiveness
and You released,
and I returned
and You covered over.
So Yours, my God,
is the praise!

I plunged into the valleys of destruction
and settled in the ravines of ruin,
exposing myself to Your chastisements
and the descent of Your punishments!

My mediation with You is the profession of Unity,
my way of coming to You that I associate nothing with You,
nor do I take along with You a god;
I have fled to You with my soul -
in You is the place of flight
for the evildoer,
the place of escape
for him who has squandered the share of his soul
and seeks asylum.

How many an enemy has
unsheathed the sword of his enmity toward me,
honed the cutting edge of his knife for me,
sharpened the tip of his blade for me,
mixed his killing potions for me,
pointed toward me his straight-flying arrows,
not allowed the eye of his watchfulness to sleep toward me,
and secretly thought of
visiting me with something hateful
and making me gulp down the bitter water of his bile!

So You looked, my God, at
my weakness in bearing oppressive burdens,
my inability to gain victory
over him who aims to war against me,
and my being alone before the great numbers
of him who is hostile toward me
and lies in wait for me
with an affliction
about which I have not thought.

You set out at once to help me
and You braced up my back!
You blunted for me his blade,
made him, after a great multitude, solitary,
raised up my heel over him,
and turned back upon him what he had pointed straight.
So You sent him back,
his rage not calmed,
his burning thirst not quenched!
Biting his fingers,
he turned his back in flight,
his columns having been of no use.

How many an oppressor has oppressed me with his tricks,
set up for me the net of his snares,

appointed over me the inspection of his regard,
and lay in ambush for me,
the lying in ambush of a predator for its game,
waiting to take advantage of its prey,
while he showed me the smile of the flatterer
and looked at me with the intensity of fury!

So when You saw, my God,
(blessed are You and high exalted)
the depravity of his secret thoughts
and the ugliness of what he harbored,
You threw him on his head into his own pitfall
and dumped him into the hole of his own digging.
So he was brought down low,
after his overbearing,
by the nooses of his own snare,
wherein he had thought he would see me;
and what came down upon his courtyard –
had it not been for Your mercy –
was on the point of coming down upon me!

How many an envier has
choked upon me in his agony,
fumed over me in his rage,
cut me with the edge of his tongue,
showed malice toward me by accusing me of his own faults,
made my good repute the target of his shots,
collared me with his own constant defects,
showed malice toward me with his trickery,
and aimed at me with his tricks!

So I called upon You, my God,
seeking aid from You,
trusting in the speed of Your response,
knowing that
he who seeks haven in the shadow of Your wing
will not be mistreated,

and he who seeks asylum in the stronghold of
Your victory
will not be frightened.
So You fortified me against his severity through Your power.

How many
a cloud of detested things You have dispelled from me,
a cloud of favor You have made rain down upon me,
a stream of mercy You have let flow,
a well-being in which You have clothed me,
an eye of mishap You have blinded,
and a wrap of distress You have removed!

How many
a good opinion You have verified,
a destitution You have redressed,
an infirmity You have restored to health,
and a misery You have transformed!

All of that was favor and graciousness from You,
and in all of it I was occupied
with acts of disobeying You.
My evildoing did not hinder You
from completing Your beneficence,
nor was I stopped
from committing acts displeasing to You. You
are not questioned as to what You do!

You were asked,
and You bestowed.
You were not asked,
and You began.
Your bounty was requested,
and You did not skimp.
You refused, my Master, everything but
beneficence,

kindness,
graciousness,
and favor,
and I refused everything
but plunging into what You have made unlawful,
transgressing Your bounds,
and paying no heed to Your threat!
So Yours is the praise, my God,
the All-powerful who is not overcome,
and the Possessor of patient waiting who does not hurry!

This is the station of one who confesses to lavishness of favors,
counters them with shortcomings,
and bears witness to his own negligence.

O God,
so I seek nearness to You through
the elevated rank of Muhammad
and the radiant degree of 'Ali,
and I turn to You through them
so that You will give me refuge
from the evil of [so and so],259
for that will not constrain You in Your wealth,
nor trouble You in Your power,
and You are powerful over everything!

So give me, my God,
by Your mercy and Your lasting bestowal of success,
that which I may take as a ladder
with which to climb to Your good pleasure
and be secure from Your punishment,
O Most merciful of the merciful!

S50 - His Supplication in Fear

O God,
You created me without fault,
nurtured me when small,
and provided me with sufficiency.

O God,
I found in the Book
which You sent down
and through which You gave good news to Your servants,
that You said,
O My servants who have been prodigal against yourselves,
do not despair of God's mercy,
surely God forgives all sins,
but there has gone ahead from me what You know
(and of which You know more than I)!
O the shame of what Your Book has counted against me!

Were it not for the places
where I expectantly hope for Your pardon,
which enfolds all things,
I would have thrown myself down [in despair]!
Were anyone able to flee from his Lord,
I would be the most obligated to flee from You!
But not a secret in earth and heaven is concealed from You,
except that You bring it.
You suffice as a recompenser! You suffice as a reckoner!

O God,
surely You would seek me if I flee
and catch me if I run.
So here I am before You,
abject, lowly, abased.
If You chastise me,

I am worthy of that,
and it would be, my Lord, an act of justice from You.
But if You pardon me,
anciently has Your pardon enfolded me
and Your well-being garmented me!

So I ask You, O God,
by Your names stored in Your treasury and
Your splendor masked by the veils!If You have
no mercy upon this anxious soul and these
uneasy, decaying bones -he cannot endure the
heat of Your sun, so how can he endure the
heatof Your Fire?
He cannot endure the sound of Your thunder,
so how can he endure the sound of Your wrath?

So have mercy upon me, O God,
for I am a vile man
and my worth is little.
Chastising me will not add the weight of a dust
more to Your kingdom.
Were chastising me something that would add to Your kingdom,
I would ask You for patience to bear it
and would love for it to belong to You;
but Your authority, my God, is mightier,
and Your kingdom more lasting,
than that the obedience of the obeyers should increase it
or the disobedience of the sinners diminish it!

So have mercy upon me,
O Most Merciful of the merciful!
Show me forbearance,
O Possessor of majesty and munificence!
And turn toward me,
Surely You are Ever-turning, All-compassionate!

S51 - His Supplication Pleading and Abasement

My God, I praise You –
and You are worthy of praise –
for Your benefaction toward me,
the lavishness of Your favors toward me,
and Your plentiful bestowal upon me,
and for showing bounty toward me
through Your mercy
and lavishing Your favor upon me.
You have done well toward me
and I am incapable of thanking You.

Were it not for Your beneficence toward me
and the lavishness of Your favors upon me,
I would not have reached the taking of my share
nor would my soul have been set right,
but You began with beneficence toward me,
provided me sufficiency in all my affairs,
turned away from me the toil of affliction,
and held back from me the feared decree.

My God, how many a toilsome affliction
which You have turned away from me!
How many a lavish favor
with which You have gladdened my eye!
How many a generous benefaction of Yours
which is present with me!

It is You
who responded to my supplication
at the time of distress,
released me from my slip
in stumbling,
and took my enemies to task
for doing wrong to me.

My God, I did not find You a miser when I asked of You
nor a withholder when I desired from You.
No, 1 found You a hearer of my supplication
and a bestower of my requests;
I found Your favors toward me lavish
in my every situation
and in my every time.

So You are praised by me
and Your benefaction honored.
My soul, my tongue, and my intelligence praise You,
a praise that reaches fulfilment
and the reality of thanksgiving,
a praise that attains to Your good pleasure with me –
so deliver me from Your displeasure!

O my cave when the ways thwart me!
O He who releases me from my stumble!
Were it not for Your covering my shameful defects,
I would be one of the disgraced.
O my confirmer through help!
Were it not for Your helping me,
I would be one of the overcome!

O He before whom
kings place the yoke of lowliness around their necks,
fearing His penalties!

O worthy of reverent fear!
O He to whom belong the names most beautiful!
I ask You to pardon me and to forgive me,
for I am not innocent that I should offer excuses,
nor a possessor of strength that I should gain victory,
nor have I any place of flight that I should flee!

I ask You to release me from my stumbles,
and before You I disavow my sins,
which have laid me waste, encompassed me, and destroyed me!

I flee from them to You, my Lord,
turning repentantly,
so turn toward me,
seeking refuge,
so grant me refuge,
asking sanctuary,
so abandon me not,
requesting,
so deprive me not,
holding fast,
so leave me not,
supplicating,
so send me not back disappointed!

I have supplicated You, my Lord,
as one miserable, abased,
apprehensive, fearful,
quaking, poor,
driven to have recourse to You!

I complain to You, my God, of my soul –
which is too weak
to hurry to that which
You have promised Your friends
or to avoid that against which
You have cautioned Your enemies –
and of the multitude of my concerns,
and of my soul's confusing thoughts.

My God, You have not disgraced me

through my secret thoughts
or destroyed me
because of my misdeeds!
I call upon You, and You respond,
even if I am slow when You call upon me.
I ask You everything I want of my needs,
and I deposit with You my secret wherever I may be.
I supplicate no one besides You,
and I hope for no one other than You.

At Your service! At Your service!
You hear him who complains to You!
You receive him who has confidence in You!
You save him who holds fast to You!
You give relief to him who seeks shelter in You!

My God, so deprive me not
of the good of the last world and the first
because of the paucity of my thanksgiving
and forgive me the sins of mine which You know!

If You chastise,
I am the wrongdoer, the neglecter,
the negligent, the sinner,
the derelict, the sluggard,
the heedless of the share of my soul!
And if You forgive –
You are the Most Merciful of the merciful!

S52 - His Supplication Imploring God

O God,
from whom nothing is concealed in earth or heaven!
How should what You have created, my God,
be concealed from You?
How should You not number
what You have made?
How should what You govern
be absent from You?
How should one who has no life except through Your provision
have the ability to flee from You?
How should one who has no road except in Your kingdom
escape from You?
Glory be to You!
He among Your creatures who fears You most
knows You best,
he among them most bent in humility
is most active in obeying You,
and he among them whom You provide
while he worships another
is most contemptible before You!

Glory be to You!
He who associates others with You and denies Your messengers
diminishes not Your authority.
He who dislikes Your decree
cannot reject Your command.
He who denies Your power
keeps himself not away from You.
He who worships other than You
escapes You not.
He who dislikes meeting You
will not be given endless life in this world.

Glory be to You!
How mighty is Your station,
overpowering Your authority,

intense Your strength,
penetrating Your command!

Glory be to You!
You have decreed death for all Your creatures,
both him who professes Your Unity
and him who disbelieves in You;each one will taste death,
each one will come home to You.

Blessed are You and high exalted!
There is no god but You, You alone, who have no associate.

I have faith in You,
I attest to Your messengers,
I accept Your Book,
I disbelieve in every object of worship other than You,
I am quit of anyone who worships another!

O God, I rise in the morning and enter the evening
making little of my good works,
confessing my sins,
admitting my offenses;
I am abased because of my prodigality against myself.
My works have destroyed me,
my caprice has ruined me,
my passions have deprived me.

So I ask You, my Master,
the asking of him whose soul is diverted
by his drawn out expectations,
whose body is heedless
because of the stillness of his veins, whose
heart is entranced
by the multitude of favors done for him,
whose reflection is little
concerning that to which he is coming home;
the asking of him

whom false expectation has overcome,
caprice has entranced,
and this world has mastered,
and over whom death has cast its shadow;
the asking of him who makes much of his sins
and confesses his offense;
the asking of him who has no Lord but You,
no friend besides You,
no one to deliver him from You,
and no asylum from You except in You.

My God,
I ask You by Your right
incumbent upon all Your creatures,
by Your mighty name
with which You commanded Your messenger to glorify You,
and by the majesty of Your generous face,
which ages not, nor changes,
nor alters, nor passes away,
that You bless Muhammad and the Household of Muhammad,
that You free me from need for all things
through worshipping You,
that You distract my soul from this world
through fear of You,
and that You turn me back toward Your abundant generosity
through Your mercy!

To You I flee,
You I fear,
from You I seek aid,
in You I hope,
You I supplicate,
in You I seek asylum,
in You I trust,
from You I ask help,
in You I have faith,
in You I have placed my confidence,
and upon Your munificence and Your generosity I rely

S53 - His Supplication in Abasing himself

My Lord,
my sins have silenced me,
and my words have been cut off.

I have no argument,
for I am the prisoner of my own affliction,
the hostage to my works,
the frequenter of my own offense,
the confused in my intended way,
the thwarted.

I have brought myself to a halt
in the halting place of the abased sinners,
the halting place of the wretched and insolent,
those who think lightly of Your promise.

Glory be to You!
What insolence I have insolently shown toward You!
What delusion with which I have deluded myself!

My Master,
have mercy on my falling flat on my face
the slipping of my foot,
grant me my ignorance through Your clemency,
and my evildoing through Your beneficence,
for I admit my sin and I confess my offense:

Here are my hand and my forelock!
I am resigned to retaliation against my soul!
Have mercy on my white hair,
the depletion of my days,

the nearing of my term,
my frailty, my misery,
and the paucity of my stratagems!

My Master,
and have mercy upon me
when my trace is cut off from this world,
my mention is effaced among the creatures,
and I join the forgotten,
like the forgotten ones!

My Master,
and have mercy upon me
at the change of my form and state
when my body decays,
my limbs are scattered,
my joints are dismembered!
O my heedlessness toward what was wanted from me!

My Master,
have mercy upon me
at my mustering and uprising
and on that day,
appoint my standing place with Your friends,
my place of emergence with Your beloveds,
and my dwelling in Your neighborhood!
O Lord of the worlds!

S54 - His Supplication for the Removal of Worries

O Reliever of worry!
O Remover of grief!
O Merciful in this world and the next
and Compassionate in both!
Bless Muhammad and his Household,
relieve my worry,
and remove my grief!

O One,
O Unique,
O Eternal Refuge!
O He Who has not begotten,
nor has been begotten,
and equal to Him is not any one!

Preserve me,
purify me,
and take away my affliction!

HERE YOU SHOULD RECITE THE THRONE VERSE (2:255-257),
THE TWO SURAS OF TAKING REFUGE (113-114),
AND UNITY (112). THEN SAY:

O God,
I ask You with the asking of him whose neediness is intense,
whose strength is frail,
whose sins are many,
the asking of one who finds no helper in his neediness,
no strengthener in his frailty,
no forgiver of his sin other than You,
O Possessor of majesty and munificence!
I ask of You a work
through which You will love him who works it
and a certainty
by which You will profit him

who is certain with the truth of certainty
concerning the execution of Your command!

O God,
bless Muhammad and the Household of Muhammad,
take my soul while it is firm in sincerity,
cut off my need for this world,
make my desire for what is with You
become a yearning to meet You,
and give me true confidence in You!

I ask of You the good of the writ that has been made
and I seek refuge with You from the evil of the writ that has been made.
I ask of You the fear of the worshipers,
the worship of those humbly fearful of You,
the certainty of those who have confidence in You,
and the confidence of those who have faith in You.

O God,
make my desire in my asking
like the desire of Your friends in their asking,
and my fear like the fear of Your friends!
Employ me in Your good pleasure
through works in which I will not leave aside
anything of Your religion,
fearing any of Your creatures!

O God,
this is my need,
so make my desire for it great,
within it make manifest my excuse,
through it instill me with my argument,
and by means of it make well my body!

O God,

some rise in the morning
having trust or hope in other than You.
I rise in the morning,
and You are my trust and my hope in all affairs,
so decree for me
those which are best in outcome
and deliver me from misguiding trials,
O Most Merciful of the merciful!

And God bless our chief,
Muhammad the Messenger of God,
the chosen,
and his Household,
the pure!

Made in the USA
Monee, IL
12 September 2024

65626570R00138